Margot's Story

As told by Elizabeth Griffin

The Lord will fulfill His purpose for me; Your love, O Lord, endures forever—do not abandon the works of Your hands.

When I heard Margot tell part of her story several years ago, I knew there was a message there for all of us. It's a message of God's tender faithfulness and provision. It's a message of hope that He has a purpose for each of our lives. And, not to overlook the fact that man has a say in all of this and that our choices often have disastrous results, it is also a message of the horrible impact that war has on everyone involved, and how far-reaching that impact can be. Though no one would argue the fault of those who perpetrate war, we sometimes neglect to show compassion to the innocent ones who are affected even as their nation chooses to pursue war.

Thank you, Margot, for sharing your story with me. Thank you, Nancy Aguilar, for your marvelous editing work. Thank you, Jan Nelson, for helping me with formatting. And thank you, Kellye Kekipi, for designing the cover.

Elizabeth Griffin (elgrif@juno.com)

CHAPTER ONE: A Godly Heritage

Tell It Again

Into a tent where a gypsy boy lay,
Dying alone at the close of the day.
News of salvation we carried; said he,
"Nobody ever has told it to me!"

> *Tell it again! Tell it again!*
> *Salvation's story repeat o'er and o'er,*
> *Till none can say, of the children of men,*
> *"Nobody ever has told me before."*

"Did He so love me, a poor little boy?
Send unto me the good tidings of joy?
Need I not perish? My hand will He hold?
Nobody ever the story has told!"

Bending, we caught the last words of his breath,
Just as he entered the valley of death:
"God sent His Son!" "Whosoever?" said he;
"Then I am sure that He sent Him for me!"

Smiling, he said, as his last sigh he spent,
"I am so glad that for me He was sent!"
Whispered, while low sank the sun in the west,
"Lord, I believe; tell it now to the rest!"

By Mrs. M. B. C. Slade
R. M. McIntosh copyright

The sweet clarity of our mother's voice filled our simple home with songs from our German fatherland. Many of them had been passed down orally through her family for generations.

As we played our childhood games, Mutti (the German name for mother) worked cheerfully to keep our home tidy, prepare our meals, and take care of us, always humming a melody or singing words that carried the traditions and stories of our ancestors down through the ages.

We loved those songs. Though our minds were too young to comprehend the messages they held, our hearts soaked up their words. Throughout our lives they would be there, a silent reminder of who we were. They held out a hope we would cling to in the years to come.

CHAPTER TWO: My Ancestors—German Immigrants in Poland

For I command you today to love the Lord your God, to walk in His ways, and to keep His commands, decrees and laws; then you will live and increase, and the Lord your God will bless you in the land you are entering to possess.   *Deuteronomy 30:16*

I believe the many unexpected mercies in my life are due in part to the obedience, and the faithful prayers, of my ancestors. Not only did they pray for their children, they also prayed for their grandchildren and those who would come after them. We can hold not only our children, but also future generations, in our prayers. This is a great privilege, and duty, that God has given to us.

My ancestors immigrated to Poland in the 1400s. History tells us there were two main reasons for this migration of people from Western to Eastern Europe. Many people moved from the Rhineland and Black Forest areas to the Eastern block countries because their skills of wood carving, glass blowing, instrument making, and other craftsmanship were in high demand there. Because my ancestors were instrument makers, they may have moved to Poland for economic opportunities. Or, they may have been moved without their consent by the reigning authority over their particular village. When a German princess married a foreign prince and went to live in his country, often an entire village of serfs was sent with her as her dowry, as in the case of Catharine the Great.

Because of these reasons, there were pockets of German immigrants throughout Poland and other Eastern European nations. In Poland, these immigrants often established their farms in groups of five or six, often in a U-shape, with a forest on one side, in front of which a communal cemetery was placed. Though living in the same area, their homes were separated by the acres of farmland they each worked, and socializing was a rare occasion. There was too much work to be done to survive on a farm, as well as the work they did as master weavers and instrument makers, for them to have any time for recreation.

Life was filled with toil. They got up before daylight and fed the livestock. Even Mutti, as a five-year-old child, had specific jobs to do—in her case, milking the cow. Every member of the family prepared the ground for planting each year, harvested the hay and other crops, cut firewood and made fires for cooking, along with all the other jobs a farm requires throughout the year. It was essential that everyone in the family worked together to maintain their existence.

My heritage included a firm belief in God and obedience to His Word. My grandfather, Christian Nebel, functioned as a Lutheran minister among the German immigrants. In the primarily Catholic country of Poland, Lutheran churches were few and far between. A farming family would travel a fair distance to attend church for confirmation and holidays, but they couldn't make the trip on a weekly basis.

Because Grandfather was educated and trusted, he was looked to as a leader in the German community. People came to him with legal issues—to make wills and deal with other legal paperwork. Though not officially ordained, he was often called to help those in need, or to pray for the sick. He taught catechism to the children in the village where he lived and the surrounding communities as well.

During winter, when the dying were not able to go to the church or hospital to be given their last rites, Grandfather was called to come to their homes and pray for them. When necessary, he also performed emergency baptisms for babies who were dying. In those days, a coffin was set up on the dining room table after someone died, and everyone in the village went through the room to pay their last respects. Grandfather was always there to help and pray when the people needed him.

The German immigrants were fiercely loyal to each other and protective. There were times when looking out for our neighbors put my family in danger. I'll never forget the story Mutti told me about one particular morning my grandfather rose with the sun to go to the market and sell his produce. It was not unusual for him to do this, and it was a good source of income for the necessary items he couldn't grow on a farm.

This morning was unusual, however. As he walked down the dirt road that bordered their farm, Grandfather saw drops of blood leading into the woods. Carefully, he and the farmhand with him followed the trail of blood to a group of men who were cooking an animal over a fire. Grandfather saw other animals tied up nearby and he recognized the livestock of one of his neighbors. Motioning to his hired hand, they both rushed from the underbrush toward the thieves and frightened them away. Then they untied the animals that were living and took them back to the neighbor.

A few days later, Grandfather heard that these robbers were targeting his family. It was not uncommon for a family to be murdered for their livestock, and he knew these men were capable of revenge for what he had done. The Polish government offered no protection to German immigrants and there was nothing to do but move, so the family packed up their household, twelve children, and animals, and moved to another German village far enough away that they wouldn't be followed.

I never knew my grandparents, but Mutti made sure my siblings and I knew about their integrity and faith. Though the closest Protestant church was in Lodz, and too far away for us to attend weekly, we always made a special trip to attend on Easter, Christmas, and other holidays. Each of us went through catechism and were confirmed in the church.

Mutti told us about Jesus and prayed with us each night before bed. Whenever Mutti prayed I knew I was in good hands— her faith never failed to be steady and comforting to me.

I knew we had been prayed for long before our birth as well, and it didn't need to be said that we were expected to walk in the faith of our fathers.

Though forced to learn Polish and use it in public, within our homes German was always spoken. This is still true for many immigrants in Eastern European countries. Because we held tightly to our heritage, in many ways we were outsiders in the country we called home. As happened with Mutti's family, from time to time we heard about a German neighbor whose livestock or crops were stolen, or whose farm had been burned down. These events made us cling to each other even more, and to our national identity. Though our people had lived in Poland for centuries, our nightly prayer remained, "Dear Lord, let next year find us in the fatherland."

It was in a valley along the river Bzura, north of the city of Lodz, Poland, that I was born in 1939 to Otto and Lydia Manthey. We lived just about right in the middle of the country. Our town of Ozorkow had recently been renamed Brunnstadt by the Nazis. The new name was prompted by the existence in town of nine artesian wells, in German called Brunnen.

Although Brunnstadt had a small population of 16,400, it

maintained four productive textile factories, one of which was the first to be built in Poland. Over 5,000 people worked in this industry, many of them German immigrants who were expert weavers and rug makers. My family included some of the people who brought these trades to the area.

The house I remember as large and beautiful was really only a little square, wooden box, and the yard likewise. It was cozy with my parents, two brothers and me, and fairly crowded when another sister and brother were born, but we didn't care. All children care about is being near to their parents. We were poor in the eyes of this world, but we didn't know it. Our neighbors lived in the same size houses and we had no one with which to compare ourselves. Within the walls of our home and community, we were content in the love of God and each other.

Papa and Mutti were hard workers. They grew most of our food themselves, and Mutti cooked it over a wood-burning oven. Papa supplied wood for this by cutting down a tree on our farm whenever we needed more fuel. On Saturday, the custom was to rise early and go with our neighbors to the nearby cities to sell our surplus milk and produce. This provided extra money for daily expenses. My parents worked from sun-up to sun-down, every day of the week. Though they never had more than they needed, the Lord always provided for us. Mutti often reminded us, "God has brought us this far, and I know He will not let us down now."

I remember how clean Mutti kept our home, and especially the thorough cleaning she did every spring. First, she would take all the furniture outside. Then she would scrub the house from top to bottom with sand and water. All our neighbors did the same. It was the German way. Children helped as soon as they were old enough to hold a brush. The day ended with many sore knuckles, rubbed raw from the grating sand. Cleanliness was indeed next to godliness, and possibly equal to it.

CHAPTER THREE: My Early Childhood in Poland

Es lauft ein fremoles kind
Es lauft ein fremoles kind
Am Abend vor Weihnachten
Durch diese stadt geschwind,
Die Lichtlein au betrachten, die angezundet sind.

Es lauft von Tur end Tor
Ich will ja gar nichts haben
Ich will ja nur ein Ohr
Von all den schonen Gaben
Die liegen Euch davor

This song is hard to translate into English, but it means something like this:
An unknown child runs through the streets of a city—a child we always knew was Christ,
At the Eve of Christmas He runs to look at the lights which have been lit.
He runs from door to gate, saying,
"I don't want any of the lovely gifts which are laid before you,
I just want to have your heart."

The message of this 15th Century German hymn is timeless. It is the natural tendency of man to live life focused on the temporary rather than the eternal. We busy ourselves with material things and allow them to distract us from the Lord. Our Creator designed us to live on a higher level than this; to live abundantly. It is His desire that we lay aside our labor and possessions, even if they are directed toward pleasing Him, and simply give Him our heart. Only then can He give us the abundant life we are intended to have, and draw us into the intimacy of relationship that both He and we desire.

This song broke our hearts as children. The melody and words combined in a haunting message, and when Mutti sang it, we covered our ears and cried, "No, Mutti. Don't sing that song. Please, Mutti!" As much as we pleaded, she kept singing it, not only at Christmas but throughout the year, because she wanted us to remember its message.

Every night we knelt with Mutti by our bedside and prayed. Then Mutti would tell us about Jesus—how he was unwelcome in this world, how he came and nobody wanted him. In my heart, I always thought, "But I want Jesus. I love him. I want to give him my doll." She was the dearest thing in my life, that doll, and so I wanted to give her to Jesus. I wanted the Lord to know I loved him.

Life was difficult for my parents, but not for me. As a

young child I enjoyed the comfort of having them with me and knowing I belonged. We were friendly with all our neighbors, German and Polish. But our neighbors were far away and we rarely saw them, so we played together. We had no idea that beyond the boundaries of our village, with the atrocities Hitler's Secret Service was committing; our German heritage made us not only outsiders to the Polish people, it made us their enemies.

On September 1, 1939 Hitler and his army marched into Poland. He did this to regain German territory lost in World War 1, and to impose his rule on the people. His method of attack was called Blitzkrieg, which means "Lightening War." Without warning, Germany attacked from the air and destroyed as much of the country's air force as possible while it was still on the ground. Then bombers hit Poland's roads and railways, munition dumps and communication centers, in order to bring mass confusion. Next, marching men were dive-bombed, and civilians were machine-gunned from the air. On the ground, tanks and artillery drove deep into the country, and the infantry took possession of the country.

As was customary when conquering a nation, Hitler's first agenda was to go to the churches and look through every public record of birth, death, and marriage. By doing this, he found out which Germans had intermarried with Poles, gypsies, or Jews. These men and women disappeared. Whether they were murdered or used as workers for the Nazi cause, we didn't know. Those who asked why this happened disappeared as well, so people quickly learned not to question. The general atmosphere in Poland was soon permeated with fear and suspicion.

The people who had not intermarried were considered "pure" Germans and were immediately drafted into Hitler's army. Because Mutti's family record showed emigration from the Black Forest area in 1450 and Papa's from the Rhineland in 1480, Papa was immediately forced to enlist. He left his job at the textile factory and began to go to the army post every day. There he did administrative work, and probably some translation as well since he was fluent in Polish and German.

I remember as a little girl feeling so proud of my Papa with his shiny black boots and fancy military uniform. He looked so handsome to me. It wasn't until years later that the uniform became a horror to me because of its association with Hitler.

Papa and Mutti never agreed with the Nazi regime, and in fact, we never used that word in our home. They just knew that if Papa refused to enlist in the German army, we might be killed or taken away. There was a pervasive fear among everyone during those years, even among Germans.

Decades later when I asked my mother why she and my father never stood up to oppose Hitler or refuse to work in his army, she said, "We were not living a normal life at that time. We were all so afraid. My whole goal was to see us through and protect my children—not to jeopardize anything." We never spoke about it as a family during the war or in the years following it.

With Hitler in control, Mutti was required to leave home each day and take a job doing shift work at the local textile factory along with the rest of the German women, so her home weaving business had to stop. Because of her skill in weaving, and her hard work, she was put in charge of other workers. Each employee had to fill a daily quota, something that was easy for Mutti to do. When she had finished her part, she helped the others who were not as quick.

Irka was a teenage Polish girl Papa hired to help Mutti take care of us. She now stayed with us while Mutti was at work. She was kind and fun, and lived with our family for five years in Poland and a short time after we went to Germany.

CHAPTER FOUR: Poland—A Country of Refuge for Jews

Not a day passes over the earth, but men and women of no note do great deeds, speak great words and suffer noble sorrows. *Charles Reade, Novelist*

As time went on, more and more Polish boys and men disappeared. I'm sure there were rumors of them going off to labor camps or being murdered, but being a little girl kept me pleasantly oblivious to that reality. Later I learned that they were used to clean stables, sent to the Russian front with the army, or made to be prison guards.

The Polish women and children who remained were suffering with hunger because Hitler fed his army first and then the German people. The Polish people only got the left-overs. Our family received vouchers to get food and Mutti would always share some of what we had with our Polish neighbors. Though it was dangerous to go out at night, she would do so in order to take food to those in need. Several times she was stopped by SS men and asked what she was doing, but she never got caught performing her acts of mercy. She would always say, "Oh, I am just walking." Fortunately, they believed her.

One day, a woman we were acquainted with from a neighboring farm came to my parents. She said, "Please, would you let my son, Janek, come and work for you? He is on the list to be taken away, and I am so afraid. I think that if he works for you, perhaps he won't have to go. Won't you please help us?"

"If we can, we'll help you," my parents told her. The next day, Papa told his commander that we needed help on our farm, and asked him to assign Janek to this duty. After much paperwork, permission was granted, and Janek came to work for us. From then on, he came every day to help Mutti chop wood and take care of all the chores.

Often when Janek left at night, Mutti would take a portion of our sausage or other meat, and sneak it into his pocket. His family didn't have enough food, and though we never had an excess of rations, Mutti had a way of stretching our food so there was always something to give. Janek never acknowledged these gifts, and Mutti never said anything either because, if the SS found out she had done this, she could have been killed. It was strictly forbidden to help the Polish people in any way.

One year after my birth in November, 1940, Mutti gave birth to my sister Inge. Then, in August of 1943, she gave birth to Herbert, the baby of the family. Our home was a busy place with five children under the age of seven and two working parents. Even if my parents had the time to think about what was happening in the world beyond our daily routine of survival during the war, my siblings and I were too young to know anything about the suffering that rose like a ground-swell in the nation of Poland.

Historically, Poland was one of the few countries in Europe to welcome Jews without hesitation. Because of this, it had a huge population of Jewish people. During the war, ninety percent of the Jews in the city of Krakow were walled in and shipped to death camps. Just south of the city by an hour, an army camp was converted into the concentration camp named Auschwitz. Over its gate a sign read, "Work Makes You Free". Four million Jews went through those gates during the war, but none of them were ever set free. Instead, they were gassed to death.

Because there were so many Jews, another camp, named Berkenow, was built. A train track from Auschwitz to Berkenow was built with a train that ran daily. Inside the camp, a German doctor stood on a platform at the end of the track. As prisoners were taken from the trains, the doctor evaluated them in order to send them one of two places. Those who looked strong were sent to do slave labor. Here they would work until they were too weak to be of use, and then they were gassed. Those who didn't look strong enough to work were immediately sent to the gas chambers.

A total of four million Jews were killed in these camps during the war. All over the country of Poland, in the middle of wheat fields, there are memorials to these men, women, and children. These stand as a cry of despair for the innocent blood that was shed, and a warning to the world of the evil man is capable of.

Three hours to the north of Krakow is the city of Warsaw. Here lived one of the largest populations of Jewish people, over 350,000. In 1939, the Nazis crammed all of these Jews into a neighborhood and built a wall around it. It was called the Warsaw ghetto. More Jews were rounded up from the countryside and forced into the ghetto until the walls were bulging with over one million inhabitants. In the horrible conditions they were forced to live with, half of the people were dead by 1942 from disease and starvation. Each day 5,000 Jews were sent from there to the death camps. By 1943, there were only 60,000 Jews left in the ghetto. Knowing they would die regardless of their actions, these brave people planned a rebellion and rose up to fight their enemies despite the impossible odds they faced. The Nazis crushed them immediately and the ghetto was demolished with all of the remaining residents killed.

In 1944, the people of Warsaw followed suit and staged their own uprising. They hoped that Soviet forces which were camped nearby would come to their aid and help them overtake the Nazis. With fierce determination, 60,000 Poles poured out of sewers and caught the Nazi army by surprise. They fought for 63 days, during which 250,000 Poles were killed as Soviet forces simply watched them be defeated from across the river. When it was all over, the Soviets marched in and took over the city. By the end of the war, two-thirds of the residents of Warsaw were dead and the city was destroyed.

Despite Hitler's claims to the contrary, at the beginning of 1945 there was increasing evidence that Germany was losing the war. Though we owned a radio, it only broadcast one station, and that station allowed only one voice to enter our house from the outside world. Day and night the German dictator yelled to the world that Germany was winning the war. After a while, my parents stopped listening. Papa had access to information from people he knew at his military post. They told him that the Russians were approaching in tanks from the East, and the allies were closing in on Germany through bombing raids.

The Polish underground movement now became more daring in their opposition. It was their time for revenge, and we often heard about German families being murdered in the night in neighborhoods surrounding ours.

The moon and stars were hidden by a thick, dark cloud the night Janek's mother came to our door wrapped in a black blanket. Mutti answered the door and she quickly slipped inside. "What is it, Marta?" Mutti asked.

Our neighbor stood silently, looking down at the piece of handkerchief she twisted in her hands. She glanced up at Mutti, then quickly back down. Finally, she whispered in Polish, "I overheard my son talking with his friends. He's part of the Polish underground." Tears welled up in her eyes as she continued, "I didn't know, but he's been doing this for several years now." Her hands shook as she covered her face. Mutti reached over to her and squeezed her shoulder gently.

After a few moments, she continued in a choking voice, "They're coming for you. It isn't safe." Mutti gasped and Marta sobbed, "I'm so sorry." Mutti put her arms around Marta and she leaned into her for a moment. "After all you've done for Janek, for us. You saved his life. But, still, they are planning to murder your family tomorrow night. You must go. You must leave right away."

Mutti just nodded, and again Marta said, "I'm so sorry." Then she left as silently as she had come.

CHAPTER FIVE: Leaving Home

"Know therefore that the Lord your God is God; He is the faithful God, keeping His covenant of love to a thousand generations of those who love Him and keep His commandments." Deut. 7:9

When Papa came home that night, Mutti stepped outside to greet him. Through the window, we could see them talking, but we couldn't hear their words. After our evening meal, Papa immediately began building three large wooden boxes. Then he and Mutti filled them with our dearest possessions—our down comforters, bank books, and birth certificates. They added Papa's wedding suit, and our Meissen porcelain cups and saucers. On the outside of each box, Papa wrote his name—Otto Manthey, Germany.

Papa and Mutti went into the backyard and began to dig holes around our oak trees. They put our silverware into these holes and covered them with dirt. Without us at home, they knew people would come and rob our house.

Back inside, he said to Mutti, "This is what we will do. You and the children will take these boxes across the border into Germany. You will go to Plauen and stay with Mr. Braun's parents there for three weeks. Tomorrow I'll put you on the train. You'll be safe there."

Later that night, I heard them praying together. Then Papa

said in a soothing voice, "Only three weeks, my darling. Then the danger will be past, and you can come back home. Then life will return to normal."

In the past, when a German family was being harassed by the government or an individual, they had simply gone into hiding for a few weeks until the conflict was forgotten. Then they returned to their home, and went on with their lives. My parents felt certain that if we left for a while, the Polish Underground would forget about their plans, and we would be able to return home safely.

The next morning, Papa reported to his post. Though he was required to spend each day there, he asked special permission from his commander to leave for a while. "I've heard a rumor that my family will be killed tonight by the underground. I must get them on the train to Germany to keep them safe," he said.

Papa knew his superior officer would do whatever he could to help his men. He was not like the SS authorities—he was a man with a heart, just like my own father. Papa was a man of integrity and his commander knew he could trust him not to leave with us. So, the commander said, "I can't give my permission for you to leave your post. You know it's forbidden. However, you must do what you need to do, Otto. Just remember that I don't know about any of this."

The German SS constantly roamed the town, looking for

any anti-German activity. If Papa were caught away from his post, he would be shot. Likewise, his commander would be shot if he had given permission to one of his men to leave while on duty.

Janek came to work as usual that day. He was shocked to see Papa at home. "We're going to the railway station," Papa said. "You will drive my wife and children, and I'll ride my horse next to the wagon to make sure they arrive there safely."

The horse was hitched to the wagon and we were already packed into the back. Reluctantly, Janek climbed up to take the reigns. He snapped them on the horse's back and the wheels of our wagon began to move, taking us away from our home. As I turned to look back, I remembered my doll. She was sitting on the white chair in our living room, just where I always kept her.

"Mutti, my doll! I forgot my doll!" I cried. "We have to go back for her! Mutti!"

"Otto!" Mutti called out. She knew how important my doll was to me. "Otto!"

"We can't go back, Margot," Papa said gently. "I'm sorry, dearest. There's no time. We've got to get to the station. There simply is no time to get your doll."

I pressed my lips together to keep from crying. My beautiful doll with her white, porcelain face was being left behind. I wanted to hold her close to me now, to take her with me. I buried my face in Mutti's skirt.

We turned the corner and our house was out of view. The neighbors we had known all our lives were nowhere to be seen. They would wake up soon and go about their daily chores, sweeping their front walkways and milking their cows, but we wouldn't be here to greet them. Would they wonder where we'd gone? We were slipping away like ghosts, never to be seen again.

Papa rode his horse by our side through town. His vigilance proved necessary when Janek stopped the wagon and said, "I refuse to go further. I won't take you to the train." His voice trembled at the stakes he faced. If he were unable to hand us over to the underground, they might take his life. He had promised to murder us that very evening.

Pulling out his revolver, and holding it to Janek's head, Papa said, "Yes, you will take us to the station." The boy sat for a moment, perhaps weighing his options. Then without a word, he drove on.

The only train at the station was a freight train filled with German soldiers coming from Russia. They were all injured, and with no one to give them the medical attention they needed, many of them were dying. The stench from their rotting wounds and secretions was overwhelming, and I felt bile rising in my throat. I didn't want to go any closer to that horrible smell, but I had no choice. One by one, Papa picked us up and put us into one of the box cars with them. It was forbidden for anyone to go on the train to Germany except these soldiers, but none of them said a word to make us leave.

As we were placed onto the floor beside them, we hugged and kissed Papa goodbye. Silently, he put the three boxes next to us. Then Mutti and Papa clung to each other for a long moment, and he lifted her onto the train. "I'll pick you up in three weeks. We will find each other. I promise," he said. Mutti nodded.

Looking my eldest brother in the eyes, Papa said, "Heinz, come here." With both hands on his shoulders, Papa said, "Heinz, you are the man of the house now. You must look after your mother and your brothers and sisters. Do you understand?"

"Yes, Papa." It was a burden no seven-year-old should be given, but in a world where twelve-year-old boys were drafted to bear arms and fight like men, no one was allowed the luxury of childhood.

Papa stepped back as the train lurched and began to grind forward. Slowly it picked up speed. As the figure of our Papa grew smaller and smaller in the distance, we began to weep. Through my own sobs, I could hear the voices of my brothers screaming, "Papa! Papa!" For one more moment, Heinz was a child, begging not to be left in charge. Then, as Papa disappeared from sight, I watched the convulsing shoulders of my brother stiffen with a responsibility he would carry for the rest of his life.

We huddled together under our feather comforter with Mutti

at the center, and Heinz on the end closest to the soldiers. "Mutti, what's that awful smell?" Inge asked. "Shhhhh," Mutti said softly, handing her a cloth to cover her nose and pulling her closer.

With the door closed, there was no escaping the stench of unwashed bodies and fermenting wounds. We sat in complete darkness, headed to an unknown destination, with no relatives to stay with, no one that we knew in Germany except the elderly parents of Heinz's former school teacher; yet, somehow, sitting there beneath Mutti's arm, I felt safe. Exhaustion from my tears, combined with the steady rhythm of her heartbeat and the warmth of her body, lulled me into a slumber that is graced to young children who are unaware of the dangers that surround them.

CHAPTER SIX: Dresden—A Center of National Pride

All the trains in Germany passed through Dresden, the pearl of the nation. Nicknamed Florence on the Elbe, it was Germany's center of art and culture. Its elaborate Baroque-style buildings were spotlighted at night so visitors could enjoy multiple sources of entertainment. At its center, the famous Zwinger building, built in 1710, housed the royal art gallery, the gallery of scientific instruments, a theatre, the opera house, and the Orangery. Its extravagantly domed assembly rooms attracted the wealthy with balls and festivities.

These and even more attractions, combined with a mild climate, brought aristocrats and royalty, along with artists and patrons, from all over the world to vacation in the Capital of Saxony. Demand for access to this destination prompted the building of railway connections between Dresden and every major city in Europe. Vacationers were frequent visitors, and many owned homes enabling them to winter in Dresden while the climates in their native countries were undesirable. Wealthy clientele supported the economy and many merchants set up cafes on the Bruhl Terrace which overlooked the river. This later became known as one of the great promenades of Europe.

The old and new town centers of Dresden were connected across the beautiful Elbe River by cobblestone bridges wide enough for both motor cars and pedestrians to enjoy at the same time. Beneath the strolling, biking, and motoring populace, paddle steamers carried passengers up and down the sparkling river.

Enlightened architectural planning produced Art Nouveau apartment houses and spacious gardens within the city, and roomy villas on the outskirts. Lovely mountains north and south of the river, and fertile vineyards and orchards nearby provided pleasant landscapes to inspire painters and musicians, as well as all lovers of beauty.

Dresden's strength in culture was matched by its powerful industry. Long famous for its white porcelain, it was also home to many modern inventions that added to its wealth. By the early 20th Century, Dresden was highly esteemed throughout the world for its production of cameras, optical instrumentation, typewriters, sewing machines, radios, and cigarettes. The people of Dresden specialized in precision work, and they were renowned for their expertise.

Despite its prosperous industry and culture, Dresden suffered along with the rest of Europe from an economic depression in the early 1930's. High unemployment brought despair to many families. This opened the door for a new leader with promises of prosperity and renewal. That leader was Adolf Hitler. Along with the rest of Germany, Dresdeners embraced Hitler because he brought hope for their economy. They were willing to overlook his questionable agendas because he promised to make Germany strong and wealthy again, as it had been before World War I.

When Hitler came into power, he capitalized on the precision work Dresdeners were famous for by transforming their factories into places that built war equipment. Cigarette machines began to make bullets; radio assembly lines manufactured communications equipment and fuses; and lens makers made highly accurate bombsights. Under the cloak of prior industries, Dresden began to manufacture "state of the art" war tools and equipment.

Mutti and Papa had heard about the great city of Dresden all their lives, but they had no idea of its involvement in Hitler's war. To them it was only a beautiful provincial city that held the greatest of Germany's artistic treasures. If that weren't enough to keep it safe from enemy attack, they believed its location surely was. As the eastern-most city in Germany, it was too far away from the West for the allied forces to attack.

The reigning optimism about Dresden's safety, combined with a desperate need on the war fronts for more weapons and ammunition, had brought about the dismantling and forfeiture of the few defensive weapons the city maintained in January of 1945.

Although the city had been bombed lightly by the allies in the previous few months, no one expected any more attacks. After all, the British loved Dresden, and along with other Europeans, often chose to vacation there. No one suspected they would seriously damage such a treasure. Indeed, the fate of cities in Germany was not always determined logically. Heidelberg was spared from bombing for the sentimental reason that it had been the honeymoon location for one of Britain's generals.

Because of the general belief that Dresden was safe from attack, the city had been established as a center for the care of wounded soldiers. These came to it in droves from the war front. Along with them, refugees poured in from the East. By the time we arrived, the bomb shelter underneath Dresden's enormous train station had been converted into a hostel for refugees and it was not only filled to its capacity of 2,000 people, it was bursting at the seams with 6,000 women and children.

CHAPTER SEVEN: The Dresden of Refugees—

February, 1945

Fear not, for I have redeemed you; I have summoned you by name; you are mine. When you pass through the waters, I will be with you; and when you pass through the rivers, they will not sweep over you. When you walk through the fire, you will not be burned; the flames will not set you ablaze. For I am the Lord, your God, the Holy One of Israel, your Savior;
Isaiah 43:1b-3a

It was in this station, to the platform over the heads of those 6,000 women and children refugees, that our train ground to a stop. The door slid open and we were able to breathe deeply of fresh air once again.

Mutti and Irka helped us climb down from the boxcar and we stretched our arms and legs in the unexpected warmth of a clear February day. Native Dresdeners refer to this type of day as "Vorfruhling", or Pre-Spring. The German Carnival, Fasching, was going on in town, and people were celebrating.

We were not there for a vacation, however, so we didn't take part in the festivities. As part of a new trainload of unwanted guests, we were pushed along with the crowd, through the city, to one of the last remaining churches that had room for refugees.

Barely five feet tall, Mutti's slight build was weighed down as she carried baby Herbert in her arms. It was impossible for her, and certainly for us as children, to carry the large boxes we had brought from Poland, so we had to leave them behind on the train and walk away with only the clothes on our backs. Walking with her, Inge, Arvid, Heinz, and I held onto the edges of her skirt to keep from being separated. Irka was always nearby. It would have been easy to get lost in such a crowd.

"Where are we going, Mutti?" Arvid asked. "I don't know darling," she replied. "We are following this crowd and I believe it will lead us to where we need to be."

"But, how do you know that, Mutti?" he asked.

"I know because God has brought us this far, and I know He will not let us down now," she replied.

From behind Mutti's skirt, I peaked out and saw refugee children running and screaming, looking for their mothers; and mothers running and calling out their children's names. Their eyes looked haunted and old. I held on tighter to my own mother, and squeezed my eyes shut as we shuffled along.

German soldiers lined the streets, writhing in pain. The hospitals were filled to capacity, and care givers were in short supply, so they had to fend for themselves. No longer useful to their country, they had been discarded here, along with thousands of women and children fleeing from Russia, Hungary, Poland, and Romania. The city was doing its best to feed and shelter them, but its supplies had dwindled to a bare minimum long before we arrived.

There were people everywhere. The press of the crowd was impossible to walk against, and we were forced to move with it, as if caught in the rush of a river headed toward feverish rapids.

After what seemed like miles, we arrived at a church. As we were pushed inside, I looked up to see an enormous domed ceiling. The ornate Baroque paintings and gilded fixtures of a prosperous time when long pews of solid oak had held well-dressed parishioners each Sunday in the sanctuary below had all been removed. Now the church served as quite a different sanctuary, its floor strewn with straw which served as a mattress for hundreds of women and children.

Down the center of the church there were long tables where food was being handed out. Settling us in a corner, Mutti said, "Children, you wait here while I go for food. Heinz, you watch over them." Her instructions were unnecessary. My brother stood like a guard dog over us, anxiously ordering us to stay still if we so much as looked in the direction Mutti had gone. He had nothing to worry about, we were holding on to each other for dear life so none of us would be lost. Though we were five children, we acted as one.

As we huddled together in that church corner, for the first time I felt afraid. There were so many people and it was so loud. The church echoed with confusion. What if Mutti didn't come back? She and God were all I needed, but what would I do if one of them disappeared? I couldn't survive without my Mutti.

It seemed like eternity before we saw her coming toward us carrying bread and some cups of milk. We all drank and ate for the first time that day, chewing the stale bread and taking slow sips of the watered down milk to make it last. Then we waited for time to pass so we could go to sleep.

The straw was alive with fleas and lice. They quickly hopped onto the new feasting ground our flesh provided and we spent a restless night slapping at them and scratching where we had missed. By morning, our skin was covered with bites. "Try not to scratch, children," Mutti said. "It will only make it worse." We wanted to obey, but the urge was too strong, and soon our skin was swelling up with red welts.

As miserable as the sleeping conditions were, we were grateful to be out of the cold, and for food to eat. Before each meal of dry bread and watered down milk, we bowed our heads and whispered prayers of thanks into our folded hands, "Thank you, Jesus, for the food we are about to eat, and please Jesus, bless Papa, wherever he is, and bring him back to us soon."

We stayed in the church for several days. One time when Mutti went outside, she saw a familiar figure crouched against a wall. The man was crying, and she called out, "Theodore, is it you?" The man looked up at her voice and she saw her sister's husband. He was from Prague, but she wondered why he was sitting there all alone. He got to his feet and they hugged and kissed. Then he said, "Have you seen my wife and children?" "No, I haven't," Mutti replied.

Uncle Theodore said, "We have lost the war. All is lost. We have nothing. Everybody in my unit is dead. I am the only survivor and I don't know what to do. I don't know where to go." Then, with urgency, he said, "Get out of this town! They're going to bomb Dresden. You must take your children and get out."

Not knowing what to do, Mutti walked back into the church, hoping to find someone to help us. As she walked back and forth, dazed at this new knowledge, she saw a man coming into the church who she knew. It was Papa! He rushed to her, and told her, "Lydia, I've been praying -- Oh God, where is my family? Are they alive? Please, show me where they are." They held each other and Mutti cried.

"I've come to tell you that you must leave Dresden tonight. The allies are going to level Dresden. They are going to bomb the city." Papa's unit was being shipped to France, and he had risked his life by leaving them to find us. "I have to go now," he said, hugging and kissing us all again. We were heartbroken to see him go, but none of us said a word. We would have to walk back to the railway station alone and try to get out of the city, but we never thought of begging him to come with us. It is a strange thing, but even though we were children, we were completely stoic. It was as if the things happening around us were too big, too overwhelming, for us to react; like we were specks of dust being blown around by an enormous windstorm. And, just as a speck of dust has no control over where it is blown, we knew instinctively that nothing we could say or do would change anything, so we remained silent.

We waited for night to come so we could walk in the safety of darkness. The city, once gay and bright with lamplight, was completely dark. Then, shortly after ten o'clock, bombs came whizzing from the sky, exploding when they hit the ground and sending debris flying in all directions. Others came down with great streaks of fire. The noise of the bombs, and of people screaming all around us, filled the streets. And, in the distance, the low hum of Russian tanks rolling closer to Germany was ever-present.

Many had taken refuge in bomb shelters at the first sound of the warning sirens, but we had nowhere to hide. Like the rest of the overflow of refugees, we were on the streets. I walked without looking about me, marching like a puppet with strings held by an unknown force. The only voice I heard was Mutti's, which I instantly obeyed without question.

Had I looked about, I would have seen images that haunted many for years to come. Incendiary bombs fell in streaks of fire, turning whatever they hit into a flaming torch, whether it be a child my age, or a horse rearing in fear. The smell of burning flesh was blocked out only by the fear that dulled my senses in this life and death battle.

CHAPTER EIGHT: Through the Fire

God Leads Us Along

In shady, green pastures, so rich and so sweet,
God leads His dear children along;
Where the water's cool flow bathes the weary one's feet,
God leads His dear children along.

Refrain:
Some through the waters, some through the flood,
Some through the fire, but all through the blood;
Some through great sorrow, but God gives a song,
In the night season and all the day long.

Sometimes on the mount where the sun shines so bright,
God leads His dear children along;
Sometimes in the valley, in darkest of night,
God leads His dear children along.

Though sorrows befall us and evils oppose,
God leads His dear children along;
Through grace we can conquer, defeat all our foes,
God leads His dear children along.

Away from the mire, and away from the clay,
God leads His dear children along;
Away up in glory, eternity's day,
God leads His dear children along.

Mutti walked straight ahead, only weaving to the right or left when a horse bolted nearby. We held on to her and to each other. And as we walked through the noise and confusion, I heard the steady voice of Mutti praying, "Our Father, which art in heaven, hallowed be Thy name. Thy kingdom come, Thy will be done, on earth as it is in heaven. Forgive us our trespasses, as we forgive those who trespass against us. And lead us not into temptation, but deliver us from evil. For Thine is the kingdom and the power and the glory forever and ever. Amen. God bless Heinz. God bless Arvid. God bless Margot. God bless Inge. God bless Herbert. God bless Otto. God bless Irka."

When her prayer was ended, she began again, repeating her petition over and over again until we came to the railway station. Though we were walking through hell itself, I felt unafraid. As long as I could hear the voice of my mother praying, I knew the arms of God were all around us.

The station was filled with people pressing toward a single goal—to get onto the last train leaving Dresden. That train was already filled over capacity, with people lying on top and holding on to every inch of its sides. Those who were strong pulled the weaker off and took their place. Their screams were shrill in the cold, night air, but no one showed mercy.

A wall of humanity stood between us and the train. It

seemed twice the height of any of us, and impenetrable, but somehow Mutti found a crack in that wall, and she led us through to the edge of the tracks. Then, one by one, she lifted us into the train. After her fifth child was on board, she and Irka climbed on to join us.

The train engine was straining. Nothing moved. It strained again without movement and we heard the dull metal clank of cars being unhooked. Screams filled the air as people rushed to find another place, many being crushed in the throng, others ripped away from the train for new ones to take their place.

I buried my face and covered my ears, but I could still hear the banging of metal against metal as more cars were unhooked and the screams grew closer. Then, through all that horrible noise, I heard my mother's voice praying again and my heart grew calm.

We began to move, slowly, so slowly that the strong were able to follow for a distance. They dropped off as we picked up speed.

Those who didn't make it were killed along with tens of thousands of Dresdeners. The military work had ceased in Dresden, but its location near the Eastern front made it a possible gathering place from which Germany could lead a renewed campaign. Perhaps this is why the allies chose to bomb it as mercilessly as Germany had bombed them. Or, perhaps it was because the destruction of its national treasure on the Elbe was the best way the allies could demoralize the German people.

The central part of the city was filled with tall, close buildings made of sandstone and brick. Underneath their attractive facades was nothing but centuries-old, dry wood. The first round of bombing set them easily ablaze. These incendiary bombs went undetected by the people who remained huddled in their shelters beneath the buildings.

When the second round of bombers came over, the city was already lit up with fire. Later the pilots reported that they could feel the heat from the blaze at 10,000 feet. Following initial orders, they dropped their bombs nonetheless, and the combined total of over 2,600 tons of explosives and incendiary devices brought about a firestorm which destroyed thirteen square miles, at least 25,000 people, and innumerable treasures and works of art. The people hiding in shelters in the historic center of the city either suffocated, were incinerated, or were blown apart. There was no escaping the powerful wind tunnel of the firestorm.

We could have been easily sucked into the inferno. There was no reason for us to be among the saved. We were no better than those left behind. We were the weakest, the smallest, the least likely to make it out. Yet, by the grace of God, we were saved, and once again, we were on a train headed to someplace we didn't know in Germany. We would be strangers there.

The prayer my people had spoken each night for hundreds

of years was being answered. We were in the fatherland. But instead of the welcome we anticipated, we were part of a multitude of unwanted refugees.

CHAPTER NINE: Plauen – February, 1945

You hem me in—behind and before; You have laid Your hand upon
me.   *Psalm 139:5*

While in Poland, Heinz had a school teacher named Mr.
Braun. He had come to our area from Plauen, in Saxony,
Germany, on what was called a hardship tour of duty. By teaching
in our school, he fulfilled a requirement of everyone in Germany
who trained for a certificate of education to spend a year teaching
in an Eastern block country. While living in our community, my
parents often invited him over for dinner, or to come to church with
us. As he got to know our family, Heinz gained a special place in
his heart, and so did we. He always said, "If you ever come to
Germany, come to my parent's house outside of Plauen. They have
a farm, and you must come and visit."

With no other connections, when our train leaving Dresden
came to the end of its line, we got on the train to Plauen. There
were no taxis or buses in those days, but because it was not unusual
for us to walk long distances, even up to 20 miles or more, we
walked out into the country and went to Mr. Braun's parent's
house. They were an old couple, with a large farmhouse, and they
took us in.

We thought that at last we were safe from bombs, but a few

hours after the sun went down on that first night, our illusion was broken. Every night after that we continued to be woken up by the blaring public alarm, announcing imminent disaster. Mutti would grab Herbert and Inga, and the rest of us would follow them down the basement steps where we would quickly cover the windows with dark sacks that had been used for coal. Without any lights, it was completely black down there.

At another time in history, that same basement might have been a fun place for young children to play; a source of the kind of spine-tingling suspense that keeps boys and girls coming back to a place of dangerous thrills. It had, after all, a huge well that opened in the middle of its dirt floor. More than once someone accidentally kicked or stepped onto a piece of coal which rolled into that well, taking several moments before hitting the water below; a reminder to us all that as we hovered below ground to escape falling bombs, we crouched dangerously close to a deep abyss.

Had we ever seen the basement during daytime, we might have liked to play in its mysterious shadows, or at least it would have lost some of its terror. But, with bombs dropping in the middle of a dark night, it held nothing but the threat of death for us. Night after night, we pressed our small bodies into the dank dirt walls, staying as far away from the abyss as we could, as we shivered in silence. Sometimes we waited for hours for the bombs to stop falling so we could go back to bed.

We were all afraid, but mostly we remained calm. Surprisingly, it was my usually brave brother Arvid who was the most frightened by this place. When the bombs began to fall, he would lie down on the damp ground and cover his face, often kicking and screaming. Perhaps he was trying to drown out the noise of the airplanes and bombs with his own voice.

One night when we were hiding, I needed to go to the bathroom. The outhouse was on the other side of the large backyard, so of course, I wasn't allowed to go. Then I began to cry because I didn't want to go to the toilet in the basement. Mutti finally said, "Alright, Margot, I will take you." She took me by the hand and ran with me to the outhouse.

Seeing us run outside emboldened old Mr. Braun. He said, "I'm not staying here any longer! I will not hide in my basement. I'll go outside and if the bombs kill me, they kill me. I would rather do that than be buried alive. I refuse to hide anymore!" So he ran outside with us.

My brothers were screaming when we left, terrified they would be buried alive, or that we would never return. We could hear their cries as we ran across the yard, "Mutti, come back. Mutti!" Just as we got into the outhouse, a plane flew very low and we heard a deafening explosion. It sounded like the world was coming to an end and we thought, "Surely in this little shack, we will die."

A moment later I was still sitting there, and we were still alive. The outhouse walls and ceiling surrounded us, just as before. We opened the door and looked out, and all we saw was a huge crater encircling the outhouse. The bomb had destroyed everything but us. There wasn't a splinter or even a piece of dirt on our bodies.

To this day, the people in Plauen tell the story of the outhouse that was spared when everything around it was destroyed. When my brother Arvid returned for a visit many years later, he mentioned the incident and they all pointed to where the outhouse had been and retold the story.

Old Mr. Braun, unfortunately, didn't fare as well. Though he recovered later, the blast hurt him badly and he had to be helped back to the house. After coming inside, Mutti said, "We are leaving this place. I must take my children to a place that is safe." The very next day she talked to people in town and someone told her about their town where there was no bombing.

Mother asked, "Where is that place? What is its name?"

They told her, "It's called Boben-neukirchen. It's over this mountain." Pointing, they said, "If you go this way, you will get there."

CHAPTER TEN: An Angel in Disguise

Determined to find a safe place for us to live, Mutti went to work finding a way to get her children over the mountain. She knew that Inge and Herbert were too young to walk that far, and they were too heavy for her to carry. She needed a stroller or wagon, but she had no money to buy one. The only thing she had of any value was a pair of boots that belonged to Papa. Boots of that quality were a lifetime investment in Poland, so she brought them with us when we fled. Taking them to town, she asked a lady with a stroller if she would take the boots in trade, and she agreed.

The next morning after breakfast, Mutti asked Mrs. Braun if we might have some bread for our journey. She wrapped freshly baked bread in a kitchen towel and tucked it into our new stroller.

Mrs. Braun said, "Frau Manthey, how will you make it? How will you take all these children, and climb over this mountain?"

Mutti said, "I don't know. All I know is that God is with us. He hasn't let us down yet, and He won't let us down now."

Then she put Inge and Herbert into the stroller and we began to walk toward the Thueringer Mountains—really a group of rolling hills covered with low meadows and an occasional oak tree.

It was frosty and cold that morning, but by noon it was very hot. It was March 27th, Heinz's seventh birthday and a little over a month since we had left our home in Poland, and it was a beautiful spring day. As we walked on the dirt paths and occasionally through the meadows that led over the hills, I picked wild flowers and made a bouquet. It got so hot that we actually took our shoes off and walked barefoot. Mutti was so happy that she began to sing one of her songs as we hiked along. We were going to a place where there would be no more bombs and we'd be safe. Life would soon get back to normal.

Then, in the midst of Mutti's song, we heard the familiar drone of airplanes. Looking around, we saw them flying low, headed right toward us. We were out in the open with no cover, like rabbits ready to be picked up and taken away by hungry hawks. Close enough to see our small frames, the bombers began to let their ammunition drop, and we began to scream.

Mutti and Irka grabbed hold of us and we ran to a house nearby. We had not noticed it before, but there was a restaurant, and it was open, so we ran into it. This was a miracle because the only people in Germany who went to restaurants were men, and there were no men in Germany anymore. Any men who were able to stand and hold a gun, from age 14 to 70, had been conscripted into the army and were either fighting or were prisoners of war. Still, here was a restaurant, open and welcoming us in as if we were out taking a leisurely stroll rather than running from low-flying bombers.

A woman was inside and she had soup cooking on the stove. We sat down and she brought us food even though we had no money to pay her. Sitting there, eating our soup, all of a sudden it seemed like the bombs were hitting the restaurant. Arvid fell to the floor beneath the table and began crying and screaming, "No, no, no!" as his fists hit the floor over and over again.

Then, as if God sent us an angel, a tall, middle-aged, German man walked up to our table. We have no idea where he came from. He shouldn't have been there. He should have been somewhere on a front fighting, or in a prison. Yet, here he was in the restaurant with us. Sitting down, he scooped all of my siblings and myself into his arms and held us. His arms were strong, like a protective fortress.

As we sat there in his arms, he began to pray for us. As his prayers filled our ears, it was like a blanket of peace was wrapped around us, and Arvid stopped crying. A wonderful quiet calmness filled the entire room.

I don't know who this man was. None of us do to this day. We never saw him again, and we weren't with him for very long. In too short a time, we needed to continue our walk over the hills to Boben-neukirchen so we would arrive before dark. The sun was only warm until three or four o'clock and then it got very cold. Still, in the short time he held us, we were renewed in courage and so was Mutti.

We arrived at the town at about seven o'clock at night, and were directed to the mayor's house. There we saw a long line of refugees ahead of us, waiting for help.

CHAPTER ELEVEN: Boben-Neukirchen—March, 1945

We'd been standing for hours when she noticed us. The nurse, dressed in a Nazi uniform, walked stiffly up and down the line of people, scrutinizing them. Seeing us, she came up to Mutti and, putting her face close to my mother's, she asked, "Where are you from?"

Mutti said, "We are from Plauen."

"That's not what I mean," she said in a harsh voice. "I want to know where you came from originally."

Mutti said, "We are from Poland."

"Get back to where you came from. You are not welcome here," the nurse said, taking a step forward to tower over Mutti.

In her steady, calm voice, Mutti looked up at the woman and said, "You know, we have prayed all our lives, 'Dear God, let us be the next year in the fatherland.' Here we are in the fatherland, and you want to send us back?"

The nurse snapped, "Get out of line and get back where you came from."

Her intimidation tactics had the opposite effect on Mutti. She knew where her provision came from, and her confidence in the Lord grew stronger in the face of this opposition. Mutti's back straightened, and she prayed out loud, "Lord, as you are my witness, I am not leaving until my children have food and shelter."

Either he heard my mother's prayer, or the Lord whispered in his ear, because suddenly the mayor of the town came walking down the long line of refugees, and looked right at us. The nurse stepped back when he said, "I will take care of these people."

He took us to the town's schoolhouse and we slept there, on the floor, along with a number of other women and children, for a few nights. When the American army marched in, they took over the schoolhouse and we were placed in the house across the street, which belonged to the town cobbler. Along with the rest of the men in town, he was away at the war. The house had a large room upstairs and a room on the main floor where he did his cobbling work. On the shelves we saw all the shoes he hadn't finished.

Another woman and her child were given the upstairs of the house and we were given the ground floor. When we moved in, my siblings and I were happy to find some playmates right away— the cobbler's shoes were filled with mice and we had a lot of fun with them. We had never had pets like these before.

Mutti, however, was not pleased with our co-inhabitants, and after we fell asleep each night, she took care of the mice. Her way of doing this was to fill a bucket with water which she then placed under the shelves of shoes. Then she took a book and used it to push the mice into the water, where they drowned. Within a few days there were no more mice for us to play with. We were disappointed, but we never knew what happened to them until

Mutti told us years later.

There was a set of bunk beds in our part of the house for us to sleep on. Mutti and Inge and I slept on the top bunk, and the boys slept underneath us. The mayor gave us straw which we stuffed into duvet covers to sleep on like a mattress.

We were immediately registered in the town. This ensured that every day Mutti could go to the mayor's office and be given some potatoes or soup for us to eat. She stood in long lines with the rest of the women, holding a pot the soup was ladled into. After a month or two of being there, we settled in a bit and were happy not to be on the move, and not to be bombed at night.

When the American troops marched in, we knew that Germany had lost the war. They were kind to the people in town, and we felt safe with them there. Shortly after that, the Allied Forces divided up the land of Germany into sections that each country would control. Located in Eastern Germany, Boben-neukirchen became part of the new Russian section, so one day the American troops marched out and Russian troops marched in to stay.

Along with the rest of the town, we were terrified of the Russians. They were known to be brutal to their prisoners, and we had no idea how they would treat us. But, as children, we were also curious about them. Because we lived across the street from the schoolhouse where they were staying, we saw them whenever we were outside in our yard or walking to the market in town.

One day, when we were walking past the schoolhouse yard on our way to get food in town, a Russian soldier came running over to us. He was talking in Russian and pointing to my little sister Inge. We backed away, not knowing what he said, and afraid that he would hurt her. Then he reached into his pocket and pulled out a photograph. It was of a woman and child, and the little girl looked a lot like Inge. Somehow, he communicated that they were his wife and daughter. Then we understood what he was saying and we laughed together. He lifted Inge high into the air and said, "You look like my daughter!" in Russian. From then on, whenever he saw us, he would pick her up.

We looked like malnourished children with bodies so skinny that our ribs poked out and our faces were sallow. Whenever he could, this soldier came to our house and brought us food. He was very kind to us. We thought he must be an officer because he told the other soldiers not to harm us, and they never did. I was too young to understand what a guardian angel he was for us, but later when I learned of the rapes that were common during this time, I knew that God was once again protecting Mutti and us.

Despite our Russian guardian angel's protection, we were still on the list to be harassed nightly by the soldiers. They came with drawn guns, always in the middle of the night, banging on the door as if to knock it down. Mutti would quickly open it and their search lights would blind us with a sudden brightness. "You fascist, you fascist!" they screamed at the five of us, along with Mutti, as we huddled, shivering in the cold, our large eyes staring at them. Often the soldiers robbed people or raped women during these raids, but they never did this to us.

It was common knowledge that if they found any evidence, even a photograph, of a Nazi, they would shoot everyone in the place. We had a photo of Papa, but whenever the Russians came, Mutti hid it beneath her blouse, against her heart.

It wasn't long after we settled into our new house that Mutti's younger brother Edmund knocked on our door. He had joined the army when he was about 19 years old, and now was 21. He had married right before joining the army and was searching for his wife all over Germany, going from one town hall to the next and looking at the registry records. This is how he found us.

Mutti and Edmund fell on each others necks and kissed, weeping. We were all thrilled to be reunited with him, even though we hadn't really known him, and my brothers moved over gladly to give him a place to sleep on the bottom bunk. I'm sure it was comforting for Mutti not to be quite so alone in the world.

Uncle Edmund soon discovered the disadvantage of our crowded sleeping conditions. Though I don't recall having any lasting trauma from all of the frightening events we went through during these years as refugees, the one incident that gave me nightmares was when Mutti and I were in the outhouse and the bombs fell. I dreamt about this for months, and every night my dream ended the same way—with me waking up as I wet the bed. Night after night, my Uncle Edmund's voice would ring out from below, "Margot! Oh, Margot!" Straw is not an absorbent material and he was unhappy to be showered in such a way.

Edmund went out and looked for work daily. He was good at meeting our needs. Sometimes he was able to do odd jobs helping local farmers, but work was hard to come by most of the time. He had an empty, desperate look in his eyes, and he often left us for weeks at a time to go in search of his wife and other family members. He finally found her in Berlin, and moved there, but not before a dangerous brush with death in our town.

It happened one day, while he was on his way to look for work, that Uncle Edmund saw a large group of soldiers at the town center. They were yelling at a line of local men who were standing in front of them. Suddenly, they raised their guns and pointed them toward the men. The women and children of Boben-neukirchen were standing on the outside of the area, watching and weeping. Uncle Edmund ran up to the soldiers and addressed them in Russian, pleading for them to spare the men, but they simply grabbed him and put him in line with the rest of the men of the town.

It was then that Mutti, Heinz, and Arvid happened to walk by on their way to the market. When they saw Uncle Edmund about to be shot, they didn't know what to do, but I am sure that Mutti began praying with all her heart. As they watched, an officer in a jeep drove up and jumped out. He yelled to the soldiers, "What are you doing?" The soldiers put down their guns, and the men from town were allowed to disperse, unharmed.

We never knew the reasons for any of this. It was like so many of the things we went through during those years—a seemingly random act that threatened all of our lives and had no logical explanation. We were only thankful once again for the mercy of God on our lives.

Outside the town was a field the American soldiers had surrounded with a fence. It had no shelter, just dirt and rain which turned to ice when the winter wind blew across it. Soon after the Russian soldiers came, we learned why this field had been fenced off. It was to hold prisoners of war.

Trucks began to arrive from out of town, carrying German prisoners back from the war. They drove up to the field and dropped the men on the ground as if they were garbage to be burned. Some of the men were dead, and the rest were wounded. Many just laid there until they died.

It became our monthly ritual to come and look for Papa

when the truck brought new men. We never saw him there, but any man who could hobble or crawl, or pull himself, would make his way across the dirt field to the barbed wire fence where we stood. Then he would hold up photographs and say, "Have you seen my child? Have you seen my wife?" We had never seen any of the women or children in those photographs.

The men said, "We are hungry. Can you make us some soup?"

The women in the town said, "No, we have no food," but Mutti said, "I have a big pot, and I have some food, but I have no way to transport it. I cannot carry such a huge pot all the way from my house to you."

With hope of a meal in mind, the men somehow came up with a child's little red wagon and gave it to her. Mutti took it home and made potato soup in the biggest pot we had, our wash pot. She put meat and vegetables in the soup from the rations we were given for our family. Then, with Heinz and Arvid helping her, she put the big pot on the wagon and, as they walked on either side to steady it, she wheeled it back to the prisoners. The men ate and ate, until they were full. Mutti came often with her soup and the soldiers worshiped her for it. She was their angel of mercy.

After Mutti was given the wagon to help carry her soup to the men, the other women in town became jealous of her. They treated her meanly, and said, "If we had known about the wagon, we would have cooked for them!" Of course, Mutti had no idea that she would receive anything for the soup she gave freely. Her only motivation was compassion.

Many women exchanged sexual favors during this time for a few extra ration cards or other advantages. Life was so difficult, and perhaps they felt they had to do this to feed their children, but not Mutti. She was a lovely woman and was approached many times by soldiers, but she never compromised her morals. She always said, "I will never tarnish the image of my husband, my children's father."

CHAPTER TWELVE: Teichweiden—October, 1945

After six or seven months of living in Boben-neukirchen, the Russians decided there were too many refugees living there, so they began to ship families to other towns. They loaded us up in a tractor and took us to another place called Teichweiden. Once again, we left everything that we had behind, including the pot from which the prisoners were fed. We were never allowed to hold on to material things, only to the Lord.

Hardest of all at this time was that our beloved Irka could not go with us to the next town. There were so many refugees in Germany that they were deporting every non-German who had come from Eastern Europe. When they came to get Irka, we all cried and clung to her. She screamed and cried as they dragged her away. It was like losing one of our own family. She had no family that we knew of back in Poland, but she had no choice except to leave. There was always loss during this time in our lives, but this was one of the bitterest losses of all.

Teichweiden is a beautiful little town with houses made of light brick and natural timbers. The people there were forced to take refugees into their homes, but of course, nobody wanted a woman with five children. The mayor of the town was the friend of the man who we were assigned to. He was the richest farmer in town and a staunch Nazi, so instead of putting us there, the mayor put a woman with one child. Then, he took us to a place outside of the community, and dropped us off in the yard of some people who lived in a shack.

After he drove away, the people saw us and locked their door. We stood outside the decrepit shack, wondering what to do as the evening grew colder. We were hungry and cold, and tired, but we had no place else to go.

Russian soldiers drove by in their jeep, making their rounds. When they saw us standing outside, they turned around and came back. A soldier yelled out to Mutti, "What are you doing there?"

"Nobody will let us come in," Mutti raised her voice just loud enough for the soldier to hear.

The soldier came barreling through the yard and demanded that the people open their door. He took out his gun, as if to shoot them, and Mutti begged him not to fire. Walking into their shack, the soldier said, "You're not staying here. This place is a pig pen. You come with me."

He took us back to the mayor, and, pointing his gun at his head, he said, "You find a place for this woman and her children to live." Mutti begged him not to shoot the mayor, but he kept his gun in place as he walked with the mayor to his jeep. Then they drove off, leaving us to wait outside the Mayor's house.

After a while, they came back and took us to the biggest farmhouse in town, where we had originally been assigned to live.

When the farmer, Walter Solomon, opened the door, the Russian soldier pointed his gun at him and said, "Now look, you must take this family into your home." Again, Mutti begged him not to shoot. Pushing past the farmer, the soldier looked around in his house and said, "This will do well. They can sleep in your living room."

To have refugees sleep in their living room was the worst thing that could happen to a German family. People never even went into the living room unless it was Christmas, confirmation, or another sacred occasion. The very best furniture was in this room, and it was no place for strangers, especially a poor woman and her five children.

"No," Mr. Solomon said. Then the soldier cocked his gun as if to shoot, and he had to let us stay.

"You bring two beds in here," the soldier said, and the family obeyed. My three brothers shared one bed, and my sister and Mutti and I another. They were the most comfortable beds we'd ever had, in the living room of the most beautiful house we had ever seen.

After the soldier left, Mutti went into the kitchen and asked the farmer's wife, "May I have some warm milk for my children? They haven't eaten today."

She said, "We don't have any food here."

Mutti came back and we prayed, "Thank You, Lord, for

your provision. We trust in You."

All of a sudden, the door opened, and a pot of warm milk was pushed into our room. It was as if she were saying, "Here, you rats, have your milk." We thanked God, and drank it, happy to be warmed and nourished.

The farmer and his wife soon came to appreciate Mutti. She had been raised on a farm so she knew how to milk a cow, kill a pig and make sausage, and plant a garden, and she went right to work. It wasn't long before the farmer said, "This woman can work harder than three men," and he and his wife began to treat her more fairly.

They liked having Mutti's help, but they still didn't want her children in their home. Things got even worse when we started attending school. My brothers and I were good students and did very well. On the other hand, the daughter of the farmer we lived with, a girl of thirteen named Sonja, was not very smart and didn't do well in school. When her parents realized that at the age of seven, I was at a higher academic level than their daughter, they focused their hatred on me.

I tried to be Sonja's friend, but she would only stand on their balcony and spit on me when I walked underneath. Her parents encouraged this, as well as calling me names and throwing rocks at me. Worse yet, they even began to turn my little sister against me, and she was too young to understand, so she joined in their meanness. I spent many hours crying over this, not understanding why they hated me.

Despite this, we had a lot of fun in Teichweiden. The town had three lakes with meadows around them. My brothers and I loved to go to these, and we quickly learned to swim because each lake had a drop-off immediately, instead of a sloping shoreline.

Everywhere we went I saw little girls carrying their dolls and I was constantly reminded of mine that we had left behind in Poland. I wanted her to be with me so much. One day, after listening to me talk about dolls so many times, Mutti took a small footstool and put a dress on it. Then she said, "Here, Margot, you can play with this. These two legs are her arms and these two are her legs." I thought this was the best doll I had ever seen! I liked it even more than one Mutti made for me later out of socks.

It was here, when I was seven years old, that I gave my heart to Jesus. Mutti had told us so many times about Jesus coming to this world, about his loneliness and his rejection. When I understood this, I prayed in my heart, "Lord Jesus, I want to give you something. If I still had my doll, I would give her to you."

Later, one Christmas, Mutti gave me a fancy porcelain doll, but I never played with her. I just wanted the one I had in Poland, my baby doll.

Once a month, Mutti took Heinz and Arvid, and walked into Rudolstadt, a town fifteen miles away, to get supplies we couldn't purchase in Teichweiden. It was an exciting day when our entire family got to walk in and have our photograph taken. Mutti wanted to record what we looked like as children, just in case Papa was still alive. But, every other time, Inge and Herbert and I had to stay at home, with me in charge. That made for a long day, as my primary responsibility was to keep my younger siblings away from the farmer and his wife so as not to annoy them.

It was a long day for Mutti and my older brothers too. The road leading to the town went through the woods of the Thuringer hills, so they walked up hill and down for hours before getting there, and then again on their way home. It was a beautiful area, but there wasn't much traffic, so it was isolated. Often young German robbers waited for people along the way, attacking them and taking their food. Russian soldiers also lay in wait for women traveling alone, so they could rape them. When they arrived home after carrying heavy bags all the way from the market, they were exhausted from both the physical and emotional exertion the trip took. Mutti always said her arms had stretched ten inches that day.

On days that Arvid stayed behind from the monthly trip into town, he would sneak out of the house and go swimming. Invariably, the farmer we lived with would find out and, thinking that he needed to fill the role of father for this unruly boy, he would beat Arvid with a horse whip. He was a cruel man, often beating his animals, as well as my brothers.

One night Mutti and Heinz failed to return from Rudolstadt. We were all worried about them, but too young to know the horrible things that could have happened. It was years later that Mutti told me the story of that day.

The morning walk and shopping had gone as predicted, but when Heinz and Mutti were ready to begin their walk home, they came across an old woman who asked for their help. She was too weak to carry her bags to the train station fast enough to catch her train home. If she missed it, she would be stranded without a place to stay for the night, so Mutti agreed to help her. She carried the woman's bags to the station while Heinz stood guard over our groceries.

By the time Mutti came back to Heinz it was starting to get dark. As they walked across the large plaza of the town, two Russian soldiers approached them and spoke in Polish to Mutti. Hearing their vulgar words, Heinz and Mutti immediately knew they were in danger, so they turned and ran across the plaza to the town's hotel. They rang the door bell and the owner answered. When he saw the Russian soldiers behind them, he said, "Get away from here, you whore," and slammed the door in Mutti's face, leaving the two of them without protection.

Heinz later told me that with all the danger we had been

through, this was the most terrifying moment of his life. Mutti grabbed his arm and they ran across the street to the police station. When she rang the bell, they could hear one policeman inside say to the other, "Don't let her in. There will only be trouble if you let her in." Fortunately, the other policeman said, "No," and reached outside to pull Mutti and Heinz inside.

If they had chosen to, the Russian soldiers could have gone into the police station and shot everyone without having to answer for their behavior, but they just turned and walked away. After they left, the policemen had a huge argument, but Heinz and Mutti's rescuer laid his coat down on a bench for Mutti to sleep on and said with finality, "She's staying here!"

A short while later, a young German man came to the station and rang the bell. When the officers let him in, he said to Mutti, "I'm walking your way. Come with me and I'll protect you." Mutti knew he'd been sent by the Russian soldiers, so she refused to go with him.

The next morning, Mutti and Heinz walked the long fifteen miles home to us. They arrived unharmed.

For the most part, our days in Teichweiden were full of work and fun. We went to school all morning long. Then we came home for lunch, after which we went to work with Mutti in the fields. There we picked berries, plowed fields, cleaned stables, and took care of the farmer's animals. They had no field hands, so we did the work. Mutti never complained, and in fact, she also did all the cooking and cleaning for the entire household.

After all her work was done, at bedtime, she would tell us about Jesus and we would pray for our Papa, asking God to protect him and bring him home to us.

After one year, our Aunt Lydia, who we called Tante Lidchen, came to stay with us for a while. She was wonderful to us, and again it was comforting to have family near. Tante Lidchen was fascinating for two reasons—she was a professional fashion designer and she was a hunchback. She had risen to the top of her profession and made gowns for royalty and the wives of high government officials. It was probably her unique talent in this arena that kept her safe from the cleansing that Hitler performed of all people who were considered disabled or deformed.

When Inge and I grew up, Tante Lidchen often made stunning outfits for us. As children, the most wonderful thing about her visits was that she had tiny models of all the gowns she had made, and she allowed us to look at them. They were fancier than anything we'd ever dreamed.

All refugees were given food vouchers at the end of each month to live on. Heinz was such a responsible child that Mutti often sent him to retrieve these from the mayor's office. A woman named Frau Schuchard, herself a refugee, had been given the job of handing these out.

One month when Heinz came home and handed Mutti the envelope, she opened it and found no vouchers. What would we possibly do without food for an entire month? Mutti said, "Heinz, there are no vouchers. Did you lose them?"

"No, Mutti. I didn't lose them. Frau Schuchard gave me the envelope and I held it tightly in my hand and walked straight home to you."

Mutti quickly put her coat on, took the envelope, and walked out the door. She knew that Heinz hadn't lost the vouchers, that he never lied, and that Frau Schuchard must have kept them for herself. She walked directly to the mayor's house and spoke in her direct, yet tactful, manner. "Frau Schuchard, you have forgotten to put our food vouchers in our envelope this month. When Heinz came home there were none."

Frau Schuchard's face flushed as she raised her voice. "Your son is a liar. I gave him those vouchers, and if he has done something with them, it's not my fault."

"My son is not a liar," Mutti said.

"How dare you accuse me of stealing your vouchers. It isn't me. It is your son, Frau Manthey."

Frau Schuchard's anger was escalating, but Mutti spoke in a

steady voice, "Frau Schuchard, Heinz never lies. We need those food vouchers, and I am going as high as I need to go, all the way to the Russian Commander, to find out the truth about this."

Suddenly Frau Schuchard looked down and said, "Oh my, will you look at this. Your vouchers must have fallen as I handed the envelope to Heinz. They are in my shoe of all places."

She handed them to Mutti without looking at her, and Mutti counted them to make sure we had the full amount.

"Thank you, Frau Schuchard," she said, and left the building.

CHAPTER THIRTEEN: Papa

I am bigger than anything that can happen to me. All these things, sorrow, misfortune and suffering, are outside my door. I am in the house and I have the key.

Charles Lummis, author & editor

We were all in the field working as usual when, nearly two years later, we saw the farmer's wife running toward us and screaming. This caught our attention because she was a lazy woman who never moved quickly. As we watched her, we saw a small piece of white paper fluttering in her hand.

As she got closer we heard her yelling, "Frau Manthey! Frau Manthey!" We called to Mutti, and she stopped working. Then we all ran down to meet the woman and she handed the paper to us. On the torn scrap of wrinkled paper were three words that would change our lives forever—"I live, Otto." It was our Papa. He was alive! We fell to our knees right there and thanked God with tears streaming down our faces.

It had been three years since we had seen our Papa. Three years of praying every morning and every night for his safety. Three years of having no idea where he was, if he was alive or dead, injured or imprisoned. Three years of knowing nothing about him. We had kept praying, but held on to only a remaining sliver of hope. After going so many times to prisoner of war camps and not seeing our father, we began to live our lives without him. That day he was given back to us.

Papa was a prisoner in the British occupied zone of West Germany when we heard from him. He was safe and healthy, but he had been to death and back during our time apart.

When Papa left us in Dresden, he had gone with his unit to France where he fought at Mozel on the Rhine. In the battle over the Bridge on Remagen, Papa's unit had been decimated. His entire unit had been killed, but he had lived. Sitting there on top of a five foot tall vineyard terrace, he was sheltered by vines, but there was shooting in front of him, above and below him, and on either side. He was surrounded, and his only thought was "I have to get out of here." Jumping down, he landed on the body of an American soldier. The soldier immediately jumped to his feet and said, "Sorry." Papa answered, "Entschuldigen," and they ran away from each other in opposite directions.

Unfortunately, Papa had no where to run, and he was captured. The French sent him to Lyon, along with other prisoners of war. There he lived in an outdoor area surrounded by a barbed wire fence, much like the one on the outside of Boben-neukirchen, exposed to the elements without any shelter. Sadly, there was no angel of mercy like Mutti there to bring any soup for Papa.

Their French captors decided to let the German men starve

to death and then claim the land of Germany as an agricultural center for Europe. If they gave the men any nourishment, it was watery broth that brought dysentery into their weakened bodies. Eighty prisoners died each day from disease and starvation. Those who survived did so by drinking the milk from dandelions and eating anything they could find—mosquitoes, flies, snails and leaves. After a while, all the grass inside their fenced camp was gone and they would reach their hands through the barbed wire as far as they could to pull grass and weeds from the ground and eat them.

The prisoners were forced to work in coal mines. They worked all year round, no matter what the weather was like. Each morning, they were picked up and trucked to these mines. There they performed physical labor until late at night when they were returned to their outside prison.

When Churchill and Stalin found out about this treatment, they said, "No, you cannot do this," to the French. Churchill did this for humanitarian reasons, but Stalin did it because he had plans to take over Germany and he wanted the men to remain alive for his purposes.

Churchill came in and forced the French to surrender their prisoners. Then he loaded the men in trucks and took them back to northern Germany where they were put in hospitals and nursed back to health in the British sector.

Papa weighed 80 pounds when he was rescued. He was one of the few men to live through imprisonment in Lyon. Later, as historians studied this, they found out something that surprised them. It was not the young, strong men who survived this ordeal. It was the older men who had families that persevered and made it back alive. The strength of relationships, and the desire to be with their loved ones again, is what motivated these men to withstand the impossible conditions they were faced with, and survive. The young men without families dependent on them had no hope and no reason to fight for life.

Papa was still a prisoner, but he was in the British sector of Northern Germany, working for their army. The American Red Cross and the Pope were working together to reunite families torn apart by the war, and once they identified who Papa was, they searched for us in order to reunite our family. He was allowed to write only those three words and when we wrote back our communication was strictly limited.

Soon after this Papa got permission to visit us. It was a complicated thing to get permission from the British and the Russians to come, but Papa somehow managed to get it. He was allowed to spend three days with us. We were overjoyed to see him, except for Herbert, who couldn't remember our father. When he had to share Mutti with Papa, Herbert got mad and hit Papa in the face, saying, "You are not my father." This broke Papa's heart because he was so thrilled to see us all again.

After another long process involving much paperwork the Russians and the British both gave permission for Mutti and one of her children to visit Papa in prison. So Mutti and Heinz went for three weeks to the prisoner of war camp where Papa was living.

While Mutti was away, Tante Lidchen came to stay with Inge and Arvid at the farmer's house, but Herbert and I were given to an old couple to look after. They agreed to take us in exchange for our additional food vouchers for the month.

This was the hardest time of all for me. Once Mutti was gone the couple was very cruel to us. Herbert was heartbroken with loneliness for Mutti and every night he would cry himself to sleep in my arms. We clung to each other and I prayed that she would come back to us safely.

Finally Mutti came back, but Heinz was not with her. He had contracted Scarlet Fever and had to stay in the hospital. As he lay there, sick to the point of dying, Mutti had to leave him. Because of his illness, the British allowed Heinz to stay, but Mutti's paperwork wouldn't allow her to stay in the British occupied zone of Germany any longer. Besides, she had to come back to her children.

CHAPTER FOURTEEN: Escape to the West—1948

Jesus said, "I am the light of the world." John 8:12

Almost immediately after her return to Teichweiden, Mutti decided that we were going to escape to West Germany. The same couple that took care of Herbert and me while she was gone also smuggled people across the border. The man agreed that if we would give him all of our food rations for the following month he would help us.

He instructed Mutti, "Take the train as far north as possible in Germany to a town on the Western border. When you get there, wait until dark and then walk on the road that leads to the border. There are trees and bushes there to hide in. Listen for my signal– the sound of an owl hooting. When you hear me, run as fast as you can to the other side until you see the light. There is an old, bombed out railway station there with a single light bulb hanging from a wire. When you see that light you will know you're in West Germany and you are safe." Then he warned her, "If anyone stumbles or falls don't stop to help them or you'll be shot."

We never saw that man again, but we followed his directions. Leaving early the next day, we took the long train ride north. Then we walked the short distance to the border and found a place to hide. While we waited in the bushes, we strained our ears to hear his sound. Crouching there, my legs grew tired and ached. Compared to my siblings I wasn't much of an athlete. I wondered, "Will I be the one left behind?" It was the question on everyone's mind. They all worried for me.

Finally we heard his signal and Mutti said, "Ready? Let's run." We took off across the big, open field. The Russian border guards started shooting at us but we just kept on running. We were like baby ducks following their Mama while hunters tried to pick them off.

Later, Mutti said, "They didn't want to shoot us. Russians also have hearts. If they had wanted to shoot us, they could have done so easily. They let us go."

The man from Teichweiden had brought us to a good place and we didn't have to run very far until we saw the light. When we got to the station, we knelt down on the ground and thanked God for saving us. We had no idea when, or even if, a train would come, or where it would take us. We only knew that we were in the West. We were safe, and soon, somehow, we would be with Papa.

We had no food to eat and it was bitterly cold. To stay warm and forget about our hunger while we waited Mutti made us run up and down the tracks near the station. After running for nearly a mile we were out in the fields. There Mutti saw three boxes, and on them was written Otto Manthey, Germany. They were the boxes we had brought with us when we left Poland. We couldn't believe it. It was a miracle. How did they get there?

We couldn't have carried them before this. In all our moving and running we had left everything behind. Yet, here they were. We all knelt and wept for cheer joy, thanking God for this miracle.

We dragged the boxes back with us but didn't open them until we were reunited with our father. Later, Papa guessed that the boxes had been left in the railway car and the soldiers must have thought, "Otto Manthey, GERMANY. Who is he?" Not knowing, they simply threw them off the train in the only place they could have remained untouched. During a time when people were taking the axe to their finest antiques in order to get one day's worth of firewood these boxes would have been burned instantly and their contents stolen if they had been found. But here they were in a place so desolate that no one ever went there.

They were only material things, but they meant much more than that to us. They were another sign of God's mercy. Just as He had directed our steps during the three years we were separated from our Papa, He had brought us right back to these boxes that He had saved for us—a little piece of our home.

CHAPTER FIFTEEN: Reunited

A train finally came, and we made our way to Munster in the Lueneburger Heide, in Northern Germany, to the prison camp where Papa was. The camp was initially used by Hitler as a munitions camp, and then for prisoners of war. Now it was used by the British to house German men. Recently it had also been opened up for the many refugee families fleeing the Eastern block. Most of these were the wives and children of the men already living there, as we were.

Papa was waiting at the station when we arrived, with Heinz by his side. My brother had fully recovered under the excellent care he received in the British hospital. They took us to our new home where Papa had been living for three years. By the time we arrived in 1948, Papa was no longer considered a prisoner of war, but was an employee of the British army as were the other refugees.

The camp consisted of wooden buildings that had been used as a munitions depot. Each of these held dozens of refugee families. The buildings were arranged in U-shapes, with a courtyard in the middle of each set of three. Within the buildings, each family had their own completely walled off area to live, and within that we put up blankets to make separate rooms and give us each a small amount of privacy. Later Papa built wooden walls and hung doors to make proper rooms.

Each family painted their section of the building on the outside and the women made curtains to hang. Shutters of different colors were put up and flower boxes were hung in front of the windows, filled with colorful flowers. After all our work, the small community looked as pretty as doll houses.

It was the happiest we had been in years. Though discriminated against by native Germans, we got along well with all the other people living in our small community because we were all refugees, thankful to be alive and together, even if we were poor. There were families from East Prussia, Schlesia, Czechoslovakia, and Rumania, all living next to us. My siblings and I had lots of fun playing with all the children. We shared everything and helped each other.

One of the best parts of being in Western Germany was that we were able to attend school immediately. There we participated in sports, music groups, and other enriching activities. My brothers were particularly popular because they were so good looking, and we were all successful in school, enjoying lots of friends.

The only trouble we had was that, for the first time during the entire war years, we had no food. In East Germany we had been registered and received food rations, but we were not wanted in West Germany. We had fled to come here, but we were not official members of society, so we had no way of getting food to eat. As a prisoner, Papa was fed, but not his family. So Papa brought his prison rations home for us to eat.

Fortunately it was potato harvest and we were allowed to glean. Mutti led the five of us to the fields every day after the farm workers had picked their crops. We would wait with the other refugees for the farmers signal, and when it sounded we would run with them to gather any potatoes we could find.

There were many prisoners who were highly educated doctors, musicians, and scientists. Many of these refused to lower themselves to glean, so they sent their children to do the work, but my parents never sent us alone because it could be dangerous.

As each person or family arrived at the field, they took a row to glean. It was an unwritten law that you never touched another person's row, and many times adults would chase away someone who tried to do this, even if they were a child. Every day we would go to another field in search of fresh crops. Sometimes we had to go up to three and a half miles to find a field. Then we would go home and Mutti would make potato soup.

In those days there were a lot of beggars. They were always coming to the door to ask for food and Mutti never refused anyone. Whether we had gleaned two or ten potatoes that day, she welcomed them to join us for dinner and simply added more water to her soup.

After a while we were registered and became recognized

citizens of West Germany. Papa worked three jobs at this point—he fixed cars, oiled tanks, and was a security guard for the British army; during his free time, he gathered iron and brass from the bombs that had fallen, which he then sold for cash; and he cleaned out the bombs from fields. These extra jobs required him to be out late, which was against the law. There was a rule that German men couldn't be out past eight o'clock, and if they were found they could be shot, but the Americans, French, and British never enforced it. Still, I worried and felt very sad for my Papa, that he had to be like a rabbit, hiding in his own land. At night, waiting for him as I lay in bed, I would pray for his protection.

CHAPTER SIXTEEN: He Never Let Us Down

*A bruised reed He will not break, and a smoldering wick He will
not snuff out.*   Isaiah 42:3

Soon Mutti had another baby, Wolfgang. Papa wanted to
give him the middle name of Amadeus, but Mutti wouldn't hear of
such presumption. It's a good thing, because out of all my brothers
and sisters, he is the least musical.

With eight people to feed, things were very hard for us, but
no matter how bad things got, Mutti would always say, "God has
brought us this far, and I know He will not let us down now."

Then one day something happened that made Mutti lose
hope. She and I had walked to the main store in town to get some
food. We had no money to pay for it, so Mutti asked the owner if
we could take it on credit and pay our bill at the end of the month.
The clerk said, "No. You already owe too much. You have to
come up with some money to pay on your bill or you cannot take
anything."

The shop was full of people who heard every word.
Humiliated, Mutti stiffened her back and took my hand. With her
head held high, we walked out of the store without saying a word.

Later that night, I could hear Mutti crying from the other
side of the thin wooden wall. Papa was speaking in a low voice,

"Don't cry. Please don't cry. You know God will not let us down now. You always say that." Through her sobs, Mutti said, "I have no faith left. My children go to bed hungry, they wake up hungry. I have to send them to school without any food. We have nothing to eat."

The next morning was Saturday and we sat at the kitchen table in silence. Mutti was there, Papa was there, and all of my brothers and my sister. We had no food to eat, but it was breakfast time, so we sat there altogether.

Mutti was looking out the window of our kitchen when she saw the mayor of our camp, an old man who was a refugee from East Prussia, pushing his bicycle down our street. He looked so tired and so old in the early light as he pushed that bike to the barracks, right toward us. On the back of his bicycle was a big cardboard box.

My parents walked outside and asked, "Herr Quastek, why are you coming here to us? What are you doing here so early in the morning?"

Herr Quastek said, "You won't believe it, but yesterday we got care packages from America. They are full of food. You have never asked for help. Everyone always comes to me and asks for this and that, but you have never asked. I don't know if you need any food, but I have made a box for you."

Then he put the box down. We peered inside and saw a big

block of yellow cheddar cheese. Then we saw large bags of dehydrated milk and potatoes, and boxes and boxes of spam. We had never seen so much food! Mutti cooked some and we had never tasted such a fancy meal. Even before the war began, we had never eaten like this.

Not only was the box full of food, there were also clothes. I had no winter coat, and there was a coat just for me. It was so beautiful it looked like it was for a movie star. I thought, "If I wear this coat I will look so rich that I will make the other poor people feel bad," so I never wore that coat. I didn't think I deserved to look so good, so I just left it hanging up. Every day I went and touched it and brushed it because it was absolutely the most beautiful thing I had ever seen, but I never wore it.

The food lasted for a long time. Mutti made it stretch until we could plant a garden and had a little bit more money to eat better. It was our personal manna from the Lord and, best of all, it brought my Mutti from despair to joy. God really had not let us down after all. Just like He had provided manna for the Israelites, He always provided what we needed.

We lived in the barracks for nine years. After a while we were given a plot of land to farm while we lived there. Mutti and we children planted vegetables and we bought some chickens. This was wonderful because we had fresh produce and meat. Mutti canned the chicken and vegetables too, so we had them during the winter months.

Later, when we were better off, Mutti sent packages of food to the farmer we had lived with in Teichweiden and to our cousins who still lived in Eastern Germany on a regular basis. She always remembered the blessing these gifts had been to us and the need that remained behind. Along with basic provisions, she sent coffee with the hope that it would somehow get through and be enjoyed by its intended recipients. The risk was high that the government would confiscate it for themselves, but sometimes things slipped by unnoticed.

CHAPTER SEVENTEEN: Freedom to Live
our Own Lives—1951

In 1951, all the prisoners were released and my parents were able to purchase land to build a house. The government paid for the materials, but we had to build it and pay them back. All of my brothers and my sister and I helped our parents build our brick house. It took several years for us to complete it. My parents lived in it for the rest of their lives and they kept the same furniture that the British army gave them for many years. Eventually they exchanged some of it and were able to buy beautiful pieces to take the place of the army issued furniture that marked them as refugees.

This was when our life really began to turn around for the good. A few years later Papa was hired to help build a defense army for Germany. This was not to be a fighting army. It was only for defense against the Russians, in case they came and tried to take over, which they did a couple of times without success. All of Germany was on alert about the Russians because we all feared them. American and other army bases were placed around Germany to help protect it, but we also needed to have our own army, so Papa helped build one.

British troops stayed in Germany until the early 1990's and American troops still remain. Through these, the Marshall Plan was instated to help Germany get back on its feet financially.

Though the allied soldiers remained in order to protect Germany from the Russians, there was an underlying hostility between the soldiers and the people. No one likes their conquerors and many Germans resented the continuing presence of foreign troops even though they created jobs. As far as the soldiers were concerned, the British and French were bitter for the losses they had incurred during the war. Only the Americans were free from lingering bitterness, and the German people welcomed them more than the others.

German men couldn't go to college because they had been closed in post-war Germany. Professors had to go under de-Nazification along with every other German male. Among other things, this required all professionals to change their line of work, so for a few years there were no teachers at the college level of education. However, these same professors became high school teachers so we really had a wonderful education.

It was a demoralizing and hopeless time for young German men. They were broken from defeat, and they walked the streets with empty eyes, aimless, not knowing what the future held for them.

During our years of struggle, Arvid had always wanted to be a baker so that we would never be hungry again. He used to say, "Mutti, I will be a baker and we will always have bread." But he was not able to become a baker because there was no one to teach him this skill.

One weekend, Papa, an accomplished chess player, was at a chess tournament in a hotel about 18 miles from our home. There he heard that they were looking for a young boy to train in hotel management. Arvid was fourteen and very short, but Papa thought that he would be good at this job and he wanted his son to have an occupation, so he told him about it.

Arvid interviewed for the job, got it, and went to live in the hotel. He worked fourteen to sixteen hours a day, carrying luggage up and down the stairs, and doing everything they wanted him to do. He had one day off a week and on that day he would ride his rusty old bicycle eighteen miles home to be with us. He was very homesick and we missed him terribly too.

One day a Swedish woman came and Arvid carried her luggage, which was as big as he was, up the stairs to her room. She gave him a banana as a tip, but he had no idea what it was. While he was staring at it, she said, "That is a banana." Arvid said, "Oh." We had read about bananas, but we didn't know what they looked like.

Arvid put the banana in his coat pocket and didn't touch it until he came home on his day off. He wanted to share it with us. When he brought the banana out and put it in the middle of the table it was brown and mushy. Not knowing that it wasn't supposed to be that way, Arvid was very proud of the treat he had brought to share. He said, "This is a banana!" and told us the story about the Swedish woman.

We all gathered around and said, "Oh," in amazed voices. So this was a banana. We didn't even know how to open it or how to eat it. Finally, we realized the outside was a peel and we opened it to find brown mush inside. Then all eight of us got a teaspoon and we each took a small scoop and ate it. We thought it was the most wonderful thing to pass our lips—a banana.

We were like that, always sharing and looking out for each other. Nothing was kept for ourselves. We had been through so much together and we remained very closely knit.

CHAPTER EIGHTEEN: Prosperity

When you have eaten and are satisfied, praise the Lord your God for the good land He has given you. Be careful that you do not forget the Lord your God, failing to observe His commands…

Eventually the government opened up some colleges. Heinz went through, and after graduating he got an excellent job. He went on to become a high official in the German government. He was always a man of the utmost integrity, and a very intelligent and hard worker.

After living in poverty for so many years, it was wonderful for our family to prosper. Each of us was highly motivated to make a good life for ourselves, and we took advantage of every opportunity given for education and employment. We all wanted to make sure we would never be in need of anything material again.

Life was so much better than it had ever been for us, except for one thing. Though we remained close to each other, we didn't remain close to the Lord. Now that we were doing well financially, we no longer turned to Him for provision and each of my siblings and my parents forgot about God. We simply moved away from Him, without looking back.

Western Germany was becoming very secular and we followed our culture. Evolution was being taught for the first time in Germany and my brothers accepted it wholeheartedly. I remember discussions around our dinner table about the foolishness of believing in God. My brother Heinz and Arvid were extremely intelligent and I believe my father agreed with them in order to keep their respect rather than because he truly believed in evolution.

I never fully accepted this new wave of thought and my sister and mother were silent during the discussions. One time I spoke up and argued with my brothers about evolution. I said, "If evolution is true, how come the monkeys don't type up in the trees?" They were so angry at this, but I just thought it was too stupid to believe—too far-fetched.

Though my younger brother Wolfgang went through confirmation in the Lutheran church, as we all had done before him, by this time it meant very little to our father. Whereas with the rest of us Papa had listened to our recitations and helped us study to pass the tests, now he didn't really care if my brother passed or not. It was merely a formality.

Mutti didn't really go along with the humanism that was sweeping Germany and the rest of us away from the Lord. She was very quiet about her faith, but I know she continued to pray for us.

During these years I also went to college and, after graduating, went to work for the German army at the ABC Institute. All the people I worked for were professors of nuclear science. They were the intellectual powerhouses of Germany and I loved working with them. I worked there for three years and probably would have continued but I wanted to learn English. I had done well in the subject at school and I wanted to be proficient.

To become a fluent English speaker I moved to Middletown on Sea near the English Channel for a year where I worked as an au pair. Learning to speak English would enable me to get a high paying job when I came back to Germany because I could work as an interpreter.

Sure enough, when I got back from England I was offered an incredible job in Frankfurt right away, so I packed my bags and took the train immediately despite my parent's pleas that I not go. After I got to the city I found out that the job had been given to someone else because I hadn't been able to call them to let them know I wanted it. We still didn't have a telephone in our home in those years.

With only five marks in my pocket, about enough for one meal, I sat down at the railway station and began to cry. As I was sitting there a man about the age of my Papa came up to me and sat down. He gave me a tissue and asked me to tell him my story. After listening to my plight, he said, "You know, I am looking for a secretary. Would you like to work for me? I travel all over the world and you can come with me. As a matter of fact, I am taking the train to Madrid right now and you can come. Would you like that?"

It was my dream to travel and the job sounded wonderful. He offered a good salary and I was ready to take it. Then I asked, "But where would I stay?" He said, "Well, you will stay with me." When I asked if he had a house, he said, "No. You will stay with me in the hotel."

Although I was terribly naive and really didn't know what he meant, I knew in my heart that this offer wasn't a good choice. Then, suddenly, I knew I had to say no, so I got up and left. I took my money and bought a streetcar pass so I could go to the unemployment office.

As I stood in line, I felt so hopeless. I didn't have enough money to even call my parents and I felt so alone that I began to sob. A young woman next to me in line asked, "Why are you crying? What is wrong?" I told her my situation and she said, "Come home with me. You can sleep at my parent's home. I have enough money to pay for a streetcar ticket for you."

We went into the unemployment office together and I met the woman behind the counter. She asked me about my experience and when she heard that I spoke English, she was elated. She said, "I think I have a job for you!" The American airport was looking for a German ground hostess who could speak English and would start immediately. "Do you want to go out there?" she said. Of course I did and my new friend said, "I'll go with you. My husband works there too."

When I got the job, one of my fellow workers overheard me saying I didn't have a place to live and she said, "I have an apartment and I only pay 30 marks (about $15) a month. Would you like it?" She wanted to move out and had to find someone to take over her lease.

I said, "What's the catch?" Most apartments cost 190 marks a month.

She said, "You have to clean the house. The apartment belongs to an old couple and they want someone to clean for them."

I said, "I can do that. I'm a good housekeeper."

Well, there were a few more catches than cleaning house. For one, the apartment had no heat, no hot water, and I had to share a toilet with five other renters. For another, it was located under the eaves of the house and there were rats. Still, it was a place to live cheaply and I was on my way.

Along with working at the airport, I began to do side work interpreting. Through social contacts I met Americans and Brits who asked me to translate business letters from English into German for them while they were in Frankfurt. To do this I picked up tape recorded letters at their hotel, took them home to translate, and then returned them to the hotel. My payment for this work was four times the regular wage of the day, so it wasn't long before I was enjoying a luxurious lifestyle.

I moved into a nicer apartment with the girl who had given hers to me when I first arrived in the city. She had lots of friends and introduced me to them. I quickly became part of an active social circle—dancing, going to the theater and concerts, and attending book fairs often during the week. On weekends I hiked and traveled throughout Western Europe. Summers were spent vacationing on the Baltic Sea.

After a few years I was hired by a large American company, Merrill Lynch. They were opening a government security division where they sold World Bank bonds and treasury notes to banks. My first position was as assistant to the director. Another man joined us with the plan of taking the test to become a trader soon and fill that role in our office since our boss was always traveling.

When my fellow employee failed to pass his test, he left. Then I took the test over the telex and passed it. With this credential, I was promoted to the position of Account Executive. Because my boss was always out of the office, I did all the trading.

I will always remember my first trade. Lloyds of London called and asked, "Can we buy 45 million dollars worth of world bank bonds from you?" I almost had a heart attack because my boss was in Rome and I didn't know what to do. So, I said, "I'll get back to you in ten minutes." I had to get in touch with the president of the company, Ned B. Ball, who lived in New Jersey. It was four in the morning his time.

I telexed, "Mr. Ball, help. I've just had a call from Lloyds of London and they want to buy 45 million dollars worth of World Bank bonds. These are my figures. Are they correct, and do you want me to go ahead and sell?"

He sent a message back, saying, "Congratulations. Sell...Sell...Sell!" It was our biggest transaction yet.

Trading was an exciting world to live in, and I made a lot of money as my career skyrocketed. Socially, I had lots of friends and was out every night having fun. My life was everything I had always wanted it to be. I had accomplished the goal of every post-war girl in Germany—I had become an emancipated woman.

The only problem in my life was one I didn't even notice. The commitment I made to God as a seven-year-old girl was nothing but a childhood memory. I had forgotten Mutti's song about the Christ of Christmas and all her teaching about Jesus. I was caught up in the success of the world, too busy to think about spiritual things anymore.

The reigning powers in post-war Europe were England and France, but it didn't take long for Germany to begin to rebuild. As the German economy grew stronger, the other countries felt threatened. After four years in Frankfurt, Merrill Lynch was relocating to London due to pressure from these countries. This move precipitated my dismissal because England wouldn't allow a German citizen to work in a trading position there.

Upon hearing this, my boss Dr. Parker said, "If Miss Manthey cannot come with me, I will not move to London." Ned B. Ball flew to London and said, "I want Miss Manthey to have this job or we won't move here." The British government circumvented their own law and I was asked to move with the company.

At the same time, I was falling in love with an American soldier who worked as a dentist in the army. Warren and I met in the spring of 1968 while he was stationed in Frankfurt. We had a whirlwind romance and he proposed in September. With two lifetime dreams offered to me, I had a decision to make–should I marry the man I loved or travel to England and continue my glamorous career?

Although I received other proposals of marriage, Warren was the type of man I wanted to marry if I were to choose marriage over my career. He was strong enough to lead a family and yet he was kind and gentle. Most important of all, he had integrity and a steadfast character.

I chose to follow my heart and we were married in January, 1969, just a few months after my 27th birthday. In December of that same year, our son Torsten was born. We lived in Germany until May, 1970, when Warren was transferred to Fort Lewis, Washington in America.

Saying goodbye to my parents was one of the hardest things

I ever had to do. They were heartbroken to have me move so far away. I remember them walking with me to the gate of their yard and Papa crying as he had to say goodbye to his grandson and daughter.

CHAPTER NINETEEN: Finally Home—1977

In America, once again I was a stranger—displaced and alone except for my husband. I had to start all over again, this time far away from my beloved parents and brothers and sister.

It wasn't too difficult while we were living at Fort Lewis and Warren was in the army because I was surrounded by other women and their children who were in my same situation. Our mutual loneliness bonded us, and actually those were happy years. But, when Warren chose to enter private practice two years later and we moved north to Kenmore I was truly lonely.

In my new neighborhood I became friends with a few other women. Soon after meeting them one became a Christian and began telling me about her faith. I really didn't want to hear what she had to say but I listened to be polite. Warren and I had no interest in spiritual things.

One day another friend invited me to attend a Billy Graham crusade with her. She wasn't a Christian, but she was curious about this well-known preacher who was coming to Seattle. When I agreed to go with her, she jokingly said, "Okay, but promise me you won't go forward when he calls people down to the podium."

I laughed and assured her I wouldn't think of doing such a thing.

The Kingdome was crowded and his sermon was short. He

talked about Noah and the Ark—about how only one man had believed God in the face of the mockery of the rest of the world and how, through his faith, he and his family had been saved. Then he calmly invited the crowd to come down and enter God's ark of salvation.

I was down on the ground floor right away. This is what I wanted, what I needed, more than anything else. There I rededicated my life to the one I had loved as a child, Jesus Christ. Then, for the first time in my entire life, after so many years of being a refugee, of leaving my belongings and my family behind, of being displaced and homeless, I felt like I was home. I belonged.

When I look back on my life I recognize that God was there all the time. Even when I was living in the world and essentially ignoring Him, I still believed He existed and prayed occasionally. When I was confirmed as a little girl, the pastor told me I was the bride of Christ and I took it seriously. I tried to live a godly life, but what I didn't know then was that you cannot do this on your own—as much as I tried, at the end of the day I would look back and realize I hadn't been godly.

I had never been taught how to give my life over to Christ. You must do this—you must die to yourself and have the Lord Jesus Christ living within you to be godly. You must maintain this relationship just like the other ones in your life or it will fade from your daily life.

I was so thrilled to have Jesus in my life again that I began to tell everyone I knew and loved. I was certain they would be happy for me and I was crushed when their reaction was the opposite of what I anticipated. Instead of rejoicing with me, my own family turned against me.

When I went home to Germany to visit, Papa said, "I forbid you to speak the name of Jesus in this house. I don't want to hear it anymore. If you cannot stop talking about Jesus, you are not welcome here anymore."

I had traded my earthly home for an eternal one and I was not going to sacrifice that for the approval of my family. I held on to Jesus and prayed.

With my parents so far away, I was only able to see them a couple times a year. When I did, I couldn't resist telling them about the things Jesus was doing in my life even though Papa sometimes became angry. I would recount to them all the trials the Lord had brought us through during the war, how he kept us safe when our family was separated, and how He had brought us back together and prospered us.

Two years before my father died, he became ill. I was visiting him and again telling him about Jesus but, as always, he was angry with me for talking about the Lord. Finally I said, "Dad, how can you turn your back on God like this? Remember how He covered us during the war and none of us was lost, and we definitely could have been lost or all wiped out. You could have died during the war too. The reason we survived is because of what God said to Abraham when He said, 'I will bless your children and your children's children to the thousandth generation because of your obedience.' We have been blessed because you and Mom had godly parents. Dad, I know it's because we had ancestors who prayed for us. God was answering their prayers. And now you have broken that link. Why don't you see that? Please Dad, my son needs his grandfather to pray for him. Dad, don't break the chain. Pray for my son. Pray for me."

Upon hearing this, my father's eyes welled up with tears and he began to weep. "I want to pray. I don't want to break the link," he said. Then I knelt by his bedside as he lay in bed, too weak to kneel. He held my hand and we prayed for him to receive Jesus as his Lord and Savior.

Mutti said that from then on my father would pray every night for all his children, their spouses, and his grandchildren. Whenever I came home to visit from America I would sit and read the Bible to him.

One time when I was in Germany, I prayed with Mutti. When I finished asking the Lord to bless so and so, and take care of this and that, she said, "I don't understand how you pray. I've never heard a prayer like this." I said, "How do you pray?"

Mutti said she prayed the Lord's Prayer and that even during the war she would pray that prayer all the time and then lift our names to the Lord. She said, "God knows everything. He knows what we need. I know He will take care of us, so I just pray the Lord's Prayer."

CHAPTER TWENTY: Heinz

I have suffered too much in this world not to hope for another.
Jacques Rousseau

Heinz was always the healthy one. "A health nut!" is what we called him. He refused to pollute his body with caffeine or sugar and never drank or smoked. Enjoying an active lifestyle, he was an accomplished athlete.

Heinz married one of the most beautiful women in Germany who had been an ice skater. They were a gorgeous couple and they socialized with the most brilliant and powerful people in the country. Their home was fabulous and they entertained often. He really lived an enviable life, but he had the same problem I'd had with success. It made him forget about where he had come from and how God had carried him through. Heinz was so busy living a lavish life that he had no time for the Lord.

Every time I visited Germany I saw Heinz and his family. After becoming a Christian, I tried to remind him of our heritage. I would get out my Bible and talk to him about Jesus, pointing to scripture and saying, "Look, here is what the Bible says."

Heinz would become agitated and say, "Don't talk with me about it! I don't want to hear about Jesus." Finally he said I wasn't welcome in his home.

I was home in America when I received the phone call telling me that Heinz had been diagnosed with stomach cancer. Along with the rest of our family, I was shocked. How could someone who had lived such a healthy lifestyle have stomach cancer? I immediately thought, "I've got to share Christ with him! I've got to make him listen to me."

He spent the next three years in and out of the hospital. As he suffered, he became bitter. When I tried to talk with him about Jesus he said, "If there is a God, why am I suffering like this?" He and his wife finally told me that I wasn't welcome in their lives anymore. They didn't want me to call or make any contact.

Then one day, Arvid called me in America. He said, "Margot, Heinz isn't expected to live beyond this weekend. You've got to talk to him to say goodbye."

I went to bed that night with Mutti's Gypsy song going through my mind. I knelt and prayed, "Lord, I don't know anything anymore. I can't talk about you to my brother. He won't let me even call him now. Oh Lord, it's just You. If you want to save him, You have to do it. You can. There's no one else."

When I climbed into bed, I lay there and cried. Heinz was a broken soul. I pleaded with God, "Don't let him die. Let me die for my brother. Don't let him die and go to hell."

After a few hours, I woke abruptly as if someone were

shaking me. The feeling was so strong that I expected someone to be standing by my bed, but no one was there. The clock on my night stand read three o'clock in morning. Then I heard the Lord say, "Get up and call Heinz."

"But Lord, I can't call him. He told me yesterday not to ever call again and his wife told me not to bother them anymore. I can't call him."

Again I heard His voice, "Call Heinz." It was such a strong impression in my mind and heart that I had to obey.

"Okay, Lord. I will call. I will talk with Heinz. But, before I talk to him about Jesus, I want to see a sign of softness in his heart. It has become as hard as marble and he doesn't want to hear about You anymore."

It was about noon in Germany. I went downstairs to the telephone and called Heinz's number. My sister-in-law answered and said, "He's not here. He's in the hospital." Her voice was very cold and defensive.

I thought, "Oh, thank You God! He's in the hospital. He has always rejected You in front of his wife and child, so he doesn't have the courage to accept You now in front of them. But maybe he will if he's alone."

I called the hospital and was put through to his room. A very weak voice answered the phone and I said, "Heinz, its Margot."

Without expression, he softly responded, "Oh, it's you."

Mustering up my courage I said, "Heinz, I want to talk about Jesus."

The weak voice said, "I don't want to hear."

Then something miraculous happened. The fear I had always had of Heinz, the awe of him as my big brother, was set aside, and the Holy Spirit rose up within me. Boldly, I said, "How dare you turn your back on God, Heinz. Have you forgotten how He brought us through Dresden? How He protected us and none of us were killed in the bombing? How He protected us as we went to Plauen and on the mountain as we hiked to Boben-neukirchen? Don't you remember how He took care of us in Teichweiden and how He healed you when you were in the British hospital? He kept Papa alive and brought us back together. How dare you forget all these things and turn your back on God."

There was silence on the other end of the phone line. Then I heard the sound of sobbing. God was softening my brother's heart. I felt so much joy at that moment that I wanted to jump through the ceiling.

"Heinz, the Bible says, "For this reason God gave His only begotten son."

"Yes, I know this," he said.

"How do you know this? When have you heard it?"

"I have heard it every day. I memorized it," he said. Then,

after a pause, he said, "But it doesn't apply."

"It does apply, Heinz. Why shouldn't it?"

"Because I'm a hypocrite. For all of my good years, I put God out of my life. How can I now, on my deathbed, go to Him? He will think I am a man without a backbone, a man without pride."

My heart was pounding so hard I could hardly breathe. "Heinz, God has given you this breath to praise His name, to commit your life to him and ask Him to forgive you. If you think that when you die your pain and suffering will be over, you are wrong. It will be multiplied. But if you ask him, cry out to him and say 'Lord, help me. I am a sinner,' the beauty that is awaiting you will surpass everything you have experienced in this life. Everything you've experienced cannot compare to the joy God has for you."

I heard his weak voice coming over the telephone wire with the firm reply, "I want it, Margot. I want Jesus."

It was the sweetest gift God could have given me. Here was my big, strong brother—the one who had taken up the mantle of leadership given by our Papa at the tender age of seven, the one who was always responsible and in charge of his brothers and sisters. He had led our family during our years without a home, and as an adult he had established his own earthly castle. Yet now as he lay dying, I was given the honor of being the one to lead him to our true home.

CHAPTER TWENTY ONE: A Man for Germany

When I became a Christian I immediately began praying for Germany. I asked God to send a man like Billy Graham to preach to the German people. Each time I returned home to visit, I saw more and more ungodliness and sin. It made me cry out, "Lord, raise up a godly man for Germany." Little did I know that one day God would call my own son Torsten to go to my homeland as a missionary.

Torsten was six when I became a Christian. He went to church with me occasionally. It broke my heart that he often chose to stay home with his father, but Warren always let him know it was his choice.

When Torsten was in college at the University of Idaho he was surrounded by the world—heavy drinking and parties, immorality and impurity. He called me once and told me he had joined a fraternity and I said, "Well, I will have to pray for you about that." When he asked why, I said, "I don't believe it's right to pledge yourself to anything but Jesus Christ." He thought I was being too rigid, as most college age people probably feel about their parents.

While in Idaho, Torsten took a philosophy class. The professor often talked about God and the Old Testament. He challenged his students with questions about how God could be so cruel as to allow Satan to tempt Job and ruin his life. He suggested that if God really existed, He had no right to be worshipped, and that He might very well be a figment of our imagination. These classes disturbed Torsten, particularly because I was sending him Bible verses frequently and he began to feel quite conflicted. He also began to feel guilty about the drinking and parties.

One day Torsten went to a Campus Crusade for Christ meeting and recommitted his life to God. Then he began asking God all sorts of questions. As he prayed, the Lord gave him a picture of a line which represented people in this world. The Lord said, "Man is down here on earth and I'm up here. Because of sin, man's destination is down here (the bottom of the page) in hell. But people don't have to go there because I've sent my son to bring them to heaven."

In this simple picture of two perpendicular lines, Torsten saw the cross and knew that it wasn't God's choice for man to go to hell, but rather for them to go to heaven. He went to his philosophy class and shared this illustration with them. Then he stopped attending the class.

At the end of the school year, Torsten moved back to Seattle to be near home and he enrolled at the University of Washington. He was looking for an apartment near the university when someone told him about a couple of guys looking for a roommate.

When he looked at their apartment, he liked it and wanted to move in. The guys were very nice and they said, "We'll get back to you. We have to pray about it."

"Are you Christians?" Torsten asked.

"Yes," they said.

"Well, that's awesome. I'm a Christian too. I want to pray about it too," he said.

They all got the go-ahead to live together and right away the boys invited Torsten to go to church with them. He went that week with them to Calvary Fellowship in Seattle and loved it.

I got a phone call from my son and he said, "Mom, you need to come here too."

That began a weekly ritual of our attending church together. We met in the parking lot each Sunday and traded Torsten's dirty clothes, which I took home to wash, for clean ones and an assortment of home cooked food that I brought for him to eat.

During Torsten's last quarter at school, he went on a six-week missionary trip to Russia. When he came back he was determined to go and serve as a missionary for a year. Both Warren and I were horrified. I thought, "No son of mine is going to be a missionary! He'll be poor and live like a beggar. He needs to go to graduate school and become a professional."

Warren urged Torsten to go to seminary and become a legitimate pastor. Even though he really didn't want his son to take up that profession, he felt it would be more acceptable that just going with no support or training. We felt humiliated at the thought of our son living in such a way.

Torsten promised to come back and go to graduate school to become a lawyer after his year in Russia was finished. He completed his coursework and graduated, then boarded a plane and headed for the mission field against our wishes.

Before he left I said, "Okay, you go to Russia for a year and then come back and make something of your life."

While he was in Russia, Torsten thrived. When he came home he was determined to be a full-time missionary but he didn't say anything about it for a while. He was living with us and we assumed he was making decisions about where to go to law school.

After a while it disturbed me that while my son was supposed to be planning for his future, all he did was go to church every time there was a service, which was several times a week. Whenever he wasn't at church, he spent all his time downstairs playing his guitar and singing worship songs. Girls would call him from the church and ask him to go out with a group, but he always refused them.

One day I confronted Torsten on his refusal to do anything social. I said, "Torsten, you will never find a wife this way. You will sit here and play the guitar until your youth is gone and no one will want you then. You must go out with the people your age from church. You will never find a wife if you don't."

His reply was, "Mom, God will give me my Rebecca. I am like Jacob. There are thousands of girls my age in Seattle. How will I know which one to pick? God will choose the right girl for me and bring her to me."

I felt so sad for my lonely son, but I gave up saying anything after that.

During this time Torsten began receiving frequent phone calls from a man in Germany. I had no idea that this man was talking to my son about coming to Germany and taking over the pastorate of a church there. He has heard about Torsten and knew he spoke German fluently.

This was exactly what Torsten was waiting for. He had been praying about going to Germany for quite a while in fact and really wanted to have the opportunity to bring his relatives to Christ.

Without talking to his father or me about it, he talked with our pastor, and Pastor Wayne immediately said, "Do it!"

Then Torsten approached me. He said, "Mom, you don't know this, but that man that has been calling me from Germany is Billy Graham's grandson. He's been working in Germany as a missionary and he has asked me to take over his church for him." He probably thought I would be happy about this since I had always told him how much I admired Billy Graham.

I was not happy at all. With no thought of this being an

answer to the very prayers I had prayed for years, I could only think of ways I could stop my son from making this horrible choice for his life.

I carefully said, "What do you want to do?"

"I've been fasting and praying and I want to go," he said.

Then I mustered up every bit of my parental authority and said, "Get that out of your mind right away because you're not going."

"I am going, Mom."

"No, you are not. I am your authority and I forbid you to go."

"Mom, my authority is Jesus Christ and I am going."

I couldn't bring myself to tell Warren for a long time. I just kept thinking that I had to find a way to make Torsten stay. When nothing worked, Warren had to be told. He was just as horrified as I was, but nothing would stop Torsten.

My entire family was furious, as I knew they would be. They didn't know what to do with someone who wasn't educated and was choosing this kind of a life. We all believed that a son of a dentist should be well-educated and make something important of his life. My siblings and I had all worked hard to become well paid professionals, and we believed that a son should do something equal or greater than his father.

My brothers called me and yelled, "How stupid can you be?

Look at what you have done with your strange religion. It is your fanaticism that is to blame for this. Your fanaticism has driven your son into despair."

Torsten was unconcerned that the family was all disowning him. His only desire was to obey what the Lord was calling him to do. In the end I had to let him go. He boarded a plane and went to the Calvary Bible College in Austria for three months—one of the most beautiful places in the world as a matter of fact. Then he went to Munich to be a missionary.

The day he arrived in the city, he met a woman named Carla who would later become his wife. God had indeed brought him his Rebecca. She is everything we could ask for in a daughter. They are a perfect match for one another, and Warren and I often think that if nothing else came out of Torsten's going to Germany to be a missionary, Carla was worth it.

Still, for months after he left, all I did was weep. I wept instead of praying.

I loved a particular book series about a woman who had been raised in an aristocratic life. She was very privileged—intelligent, well-educated, played the piano well enough to be a concert pianist, and she was beautiful. Then, when she had grown up, she became a Christian. She went to her parents and told them she wanted to go to China as a missionary. They were horrified, just as I was with Torsten. She went anyway, just like my son.

And, in China, she lived with horrible conditions, even to the point of having rats in her home.

I loved this woman's life story and admired her very much. But, even as I read it, I thought, "I hope my son doesn't become like that."

I prayed, "Lord, when I asked You to raise somebody up for Germany, I didn't mean my son. That isn't part of the bargain."

One day I went to my prayer group with four other women and I was crying. As we prayed, I cried about Torsten's decision to go to Germany. Another woman was there whose son was addicted to drugs and alcohol. She looked at me and said, "What are you saying? I would give my right arm to have my son doing that."

That made me stop and think for the first time since Torsten had left. I thought, "What am I doing? Why am I so disagreeable and ungrateful? I should support Torsten and not criticize." I repented of my attitude and my heart became peaceful.

As my Bible study teacher always said, "Salvation is free, but to follow Christ is a big cost. It will cost you everything."

When I was a child, we were very poor, but it didn't matter. Everybody was in the same boat, especially during the war. That made it easier to accept because poverty was beyond our control, rather than being anything we chose. We all lived with the dream of becoming rich one day.

When I became an adult, I was rich compared to those early days in my life. Though not among the wealthiest in the world, my husband and I always had a comfortable life and we were able to give our son everything he needed and more. Yet, when our son grew up, he chose to live differently than the world does. Instead of seeking material riches, he chose to seek spiritual wealth.

I think of Torsten and Carla, and the two boys they have now and I feel so grateful for their lives. Though I am tempted sometimes to worry about their finances, to wish they had an easier life, I look at the sons and daughters my friends have—people who have everything material this world could offer and yet are divorced or raising other people's children, and I know my son and his wife are truly the wealthy ones. Torsten made the better choice for his life.

In other ways than material, being a follower of Christ has cost me much during my lifetime. It cost me the respect of my family, peace in my marriage, and brought the ridicule of many— yet I wouldn't trade it for anything. Not only is Jesus the one who gives my life meaning and fulfillment now, I also have eternal salvation; and heaven will be the ultimate blessing, beyond anything I could ever imagine.

APPENDIX 1: A brief history of WW2
Invasion of Poland and Hitler's Plan

If we could read the secret history of our enemies we should find in each man's life sorrow and suffering enough to disarm all hostility.
Longfellow

On September 1, 1939 Hitler invaded Poland. He did this to regain German territory lost in World War 1, and to impose his rule on the people. His method of attack was called Blitzkrieg, which means "Lightening War". Without warning, Germany attacked from the air and destroyed as much of the country's air force as possible while it was still on the ground. Then bombers hit Poland's roads and railways, munition dumps and communication centers, in order to bring mass confusion. Thirdly, marching men were dive-bombed, and civilian refugees were machine-gunned from the air. On the ground, tanks and artillery drove deep into the country, and the infantry took possession of the country.

The Polish people fought fiercely to defend their land, but their outdated weapons and small numbers were no match against the German army. Still, it took days, and in some cases, weeks, to overcome cities the dictator thought would be subdued in hours.

Following the army, Hitler sent his SS men to terrorize the people into complete submission. Their job was to annihilate

Polish society, and everyone who didn't support Nazism, and they never followed the rules of war. Several army commanders criticized the Fuhrer for these tactics, but it was to no avail. In Germany, those who voiced their disagreement were imprisoned along with the rest of the victims of war. The people quickly learned that to oppose Hitler meant death.

Unbeknownst to the rest of the world, Hitler made an alliance with Russia one week before invading Poland. This gave the Soviets the Eastern part of Poland. It was his plan to take the East back later, but for now he feigned peace with Russia so that he would only have to fight on one front at a time. Suddenly the people of Poland found themselves under either German or Russian rule, and their government was in exile.

Everyone who wasn't what Hitler considered a "pure" Aryan was in danger. Ultimately, this included everyone not of pure German descent. In practice it also included those within this category who had physical or mental disabilities, and political persuasions or ethics that differed from the Nazi regime. While Jews, Gypsies and Poles were being killed, the Fuhrer gave orders for the populations of conquered countries and of Germany itself, to be cleansed of the senile, insane, and non-German. Hospitals were set up to euthanize anyone considered "defective"—defined as anyone who fit into one of these categories, including newborn babies with abnormalities, or anyone who disagreed with Hitler.

A man named John Galsworthy said, "Once admit that we have the right to inflict unnecessary suffering and you destroy the very basis of human society." This is exactly what Hitler intended to do. He intended to destroy all those he considered unworthy of life—all those who were not like himself. Because of his insanity he considered this a necessary act. The question that remains unanswered is, "How did he convince the men and women who followed him that the suffering they inflicted was necessary?"

Those who followed his orders learned not to hesitate to take a life, not to feel pity or compassion, not to feel anything but a superiority which gave them the right to destroy people at will. Those who refused to accept this ideology were in the way of progress and their extermination along with the rest was necessary in order that a superior race and world could be formed.

Along with annihilating the unacceptable, Hitler's plan to create a perfect race of people included sequestering girls with pure German bloodlines and having them impregnated in order to produce this race and populate a new society.

The common people in Germany, and in its conquered countries, knew nothing about this master plan. All they knew was that even if they were lucky enough to be the acceptable race, many of their neighbors were disappearing and it wasn't safe to ask why.

Though the people of Poland surrendered, they never fully

gave up. There was an underground resistance movement that operated throughout the war and the government maintained its national status in exile, waiting for the day it would be able to come back and take its place of power again.

BIBLIOGRAPHY

1. Escape to West Berlin, Maurine F. Dahlberg Farrar, Straus and Giroux/New York; 2004.
2. Memories of WW II and It's Aftermath, Inge E. Stanneck Gross, Island in the Sky Publishing Co.; Eastsound, WA 2005
3. Poland in World War II, An Illustrated Military History, Andrew Hempel, Hippocrene Books, Inc., New York, 2000.
4. Dresden: Tuesday, February 13, 1945, Frederick Taylor, Harper Collins Publishers, New York, 2004.
5. A Thread of Grace Mary Doria Russell
6. Germany Profiled: Essential Facts on society, business and politics in Germany Edited by Barry Turner St. Martin's Press, NY 1999
7. The German Way: Aspects of Behavior, Attitudes, and Customs in the German-speaking World, Hyde Flippo, Passport Books, NTC/Contemporary Publishing Group, Chicago, Illinois 1999
8. An Uncertain Hour: The French, The Germans, the Jews, the Klaus Barbie Trial, and the City of Lyon, 1940-1945, Ted Morgan, Arbor House/William Morrow, NY 1990
9. Dietrich Bonhoeffer's Prison Poems, Editor and Translator Edwin Robertson, Zondervan, Grand Rapids, Michigan 1999
10. World War 2 Chronicles: From D-Day to V-E Day, Julie Klam, Smart Apple Media, Minnesota, 1980.
11. Worship In Song, A. T. Hardy, Music Editor, Light and Life Press, Winona Lake, Indiana, 1935.
12. Great Hymns of the Faith, compiled and edited by John W. Peterson, Zondervan Publishing House, Grand Rapids, Michigan, 1971.

7110758R00076

Made in the USA
San Bernardino, CA
21 December 2013